C000064283

LET'S PRAISE

Let's Praise Him Again!

EDITED BY JOEL EDWARDS

KINGSWAY PUBLICATIONS
EASTBOURNE

Copyright © Joel Edwards 1992
The right of Joel Edwards to be identified
as author of this work has been asserted by him in
accordance with the Copyright, Design
and Patents Act 1988.

First published 1992.

All rights reserved.
No part of this publication may be reproduced or
transmitted in any form or by any means, electronic
or mechanical, including photocopy, recording, or any
information storage and retrieval system, without
permission in writing from the publisher.

Unless otherwise indicated, biblical quotations are from the
New International Version © 1973, 1978, 1984 by the
International Bible Society.

Cover design by Tony Carr Designs

ISBN 0 85476 306 6

Printed in Great Britain for
KINGSWAY PUBLICATIONS LTD
Lottbridge Drove, Eastbourne, E Sussex BN23 6NT by
Clays Ltd, St. Ives plc.
Typeset by J&L Composition Ltd, Filey, North Yorkshire

Contents

Foreword

by Roger Forster

One of the greatest compliments ever be paid to me was by Joel Edwards. Introducing my pale Anglo-Saxon visage to a very ethnically mixed congregation in East London he said, "We sure like Roger's preaching. He preaches like a black man." When the laughter had died down he added, "He preaches a long time." At this remark the laughter, led by the Afro-Caribbeans, was even longer (than the preach, I mean, of course!).

With equal verbal ease on paper as in the pulpit, Joel, with the help of his three friends, examines, explores, assesses, and for some will introduce for the first time, the richness of Afro-Caribbean worship and church leadership style.

These two functions of worship and leadership are to all intents and purposes one. The black leader leads by preaching and the preacher is the chief worshipper. This and many other insights will challenge us and, if taken on board in other traditions, will enrich worship throughout the Christian church. Already black music, nurtured, developed and forged in revival fire and in a church which wore the mark of a true church, namely suffering, has spread throughout the secular world, creating in the younger generation, if not all our current generations, a common cultural ethos which is being employed by musicians to communicate the gospel message. We must not leave this advantage of a world music culture to be exploited by the secular entertainers. The black church has given us an international language to facilitate world evangelisation. We, from all races and languages, must utilise it. The 60s saw the Beatles become the prophets of the decade. If we had been true to the musical roots it could have been Jesus who was heard. Don't let us give this gift away in our decade, nor in all of Joel's humble self-criticisms of his culture miss this inter-cultural, cross-cultural contribution his black-culture church has given us all.

"I'm glad I've got a God I can feel," cries a black preacher in worship. This is not far from Wesley's aspirations as a Church of England clergyman before his evangelical conversion: "I want to feel that I believe." "When you've been to a black church you know you've been," is hardly foreign for any worshipping community when at its heart it is seeking God. "We fell on our faces in the presence of his majesty," was the experience that led to the evangelical awakening of the eighteenth century. Congregational participation is a New Testament ideal, as is seen in 1 Corinthians 14:26: "What then shall we say, brothers? When you come together, everyone has a hymn, or a word of instruction, a revelation, a tongue, or an interpretation." This is a scriptural description of a meeting which no church should feel is alien. The black churches have often led the way in total congregational participation. The church is meant to be owned by all. This is one way of ensuring it is.

Now, I don't want to rewrite Joel's book for him—his is too good to attempt such a thing. Neither must I "preach a long time" despite his encouragement. This is one, if not the best, popular introduction and enquiry into the black worship experience, and many people will be helped by it—black, white, and indeed any other variation in God's multi-coloured world. Many questions are raised, including multi-cultural congregations, with which our own fellowship in Ichthus is grappling. In what is still a fairly predominantly Anglo-Saxon church we have integrated leadership, mixed cultural worship, and we belong to the Afro-Caribbean Evangelical Alliance. This is because we want to be in what

God is doing and not miss out on the treasures unearthed by our black brothers and sisters. Consider Revelation 5:9–10:

> You are worthy to take the scroll and open its seals, because you were slain, and with your blood you purchased men for God from every tribe and language and people and nation. You have made them to be a kingdom and priests to serve our God, and they will reign on the earth.

This passage gives us beautiful vision, not only of the future, but even for the present. If we can't worship together now, what makes us think we shall worship together then, when all the nations bring their glory to Jerusalem and add it to the glory of God (Rev. 21:11, 26)? How can such things be? Let's wait and see while we fulfil the Scriptures which enjoin integrated worship:

> Again it says,
> "Rejoice, Gentiles, *with* his people."
> And again,
> "Praise the Lord, *all* you Gentiles,
> and sing praises to him, all you peoples." (Rom. 15:10–11, my italics)

Currently I am white, but who knows what I'll be in the resurrection—we are not told. Perhaps we'll all be mixed up colour-wise. It would be good if we were all different from our present pigmentation. We will have a glorious body anyhow, so we'd better mix and match now. Well, we can mix, but can we match the colour, exuberance, fire and experience of Christ that the black churches have and still offer to us all?

When black Pastor Seymour prayed with his congregation in Azuza Street in 1906 they said you could feel the love of God within a quarter of a mile of the building. May I say to the black-led, black and integrated churches, go on leading, praying, worshipping. We all need that love; we all need that God.

Introduction

Every so often a new development takes place in human history which was neither planned nor anticipated and which falls outside the normal sequence of events. When it does, we are apt to give it the name 'phenomenon'. Such an event has been the relatively rapid growth of what has been known as the black church or black-led church in Britain over the last forty years.

Inevitably, a phenomenon becomes the subject of curiosity and investigation. This indeed has been the lot of the black church community as it has been catalogued, described and analysed by fellow Christians and social scientists who have been impressed or bemused. Only in more recent years have black church leaders begun the process of reflection and telling the story of this phenomenon from our own perspective. *Let's Praise Him Again* is another contribution to the *inside story* of the black church community.

This book has emerged from a unique forum of Christians who attended the Afro-Caribbean Evangelical Alliance theological study group in December 1989 to discuss the subject of worship specifically from an Afro-Caribbean perspective. This book does not claim to be the comprehensive account of Afro-Caribbean worship. Rather it seeks to expand the initial thoughts of the conference. We are aware of the glaring omissions of any significant references to the experience of the growing African and Asian churches. Such an inclusion was not the remit of this exercise, although we recognise the validity and complementary nature of those cultural experiences.

In this brief outline, we have tried to present an open account of the Afro-Caribbean worship setting and attempted to be both descriptive and reflective. We do not guarantee that everyone will find it agreeable, though neither does this book set out to be disagreeable. The first chapter, 'Black, Black-led or What?', attempts to deal with the question of identification and raise relevant issues about the implications of the 'black' or 'black-led' church.

An introductory chapter on worship then outlines some basic points about worship ('Biblical Worship'). Admittedly much of the information contained in it can be found in numerous other books, but it is an integral part of this book for two reasons. First, it shows our commitment to an 'objective' and Bible-based appreciation of worship. While we have an experience of worship that comes from a particular cultural milieu, such worship must be rooted in an understanding of what the Bible says about worship. As far as possible, worship should be measured against a biblical culture of worship. Perhaps some readers may turn to this book because it relates to their cultural situation. In the event that such persons have never looked at another book on the subject, I do hope this chapter will help to provide an objective biblical point of reference.

'The Pulpit Response to Worship', Chapter 3, attempts an outline of the black preacher's central role as a worship leader and the responsibility laid on him to define the distinctions between cultural baggage and biblical worship that may be culturally experienced and expressed.

There is a common assumption that black church is synonymous with Pentecostal. That is far from the truth, though undoubtedly the black church community is substantially Pentecostal. 'The Pentecostal Distinctives', Chapter 4, next presents a profile of black Pentecostalism. (A more exhaustive comparison with 'white-led' Pentecostalism would be a fascinating exercise but was not the intention of this chapter.)

Our final chapter, on cultural dynamics, puts the issue of Afro-Caribbean worship within the wider context of cultural transitions. It attempts a cursory examination of the meaning and impact of culture on the worship setting and raises some significant points for the future of the Afro-Caribbean cultural expression of worship.

If this book does not answer all the questions it raises it will still have been worthwhile if we help both black and white Christians at least to identify those questions more clearly.

Joel Edwards

I

Black, Black-led or What?

Arlington Trotman

Whose identity?

There is increasing awareness in Britain of the dishar-
mony between blacks and whites that prevents the black
church community from taking its full place and exert-
ing a greater influence within the wider church community. To a large degree the black church community
has been placed in a second-class and marginal context,
and at the heart of this situation lies the issue of race.
Such awareness has developed not only among Britain's
blacks, but also in the United States of America and the
Caribbean. One of the more significant results of this
protracted marginalisation, has been its particularly negative effect on the identity of Afro-Caribbean Christians,
and the lack of appreciation of the spiritual challenge
they represent. Worship within the so-called 'black-led'
church, as it has come to be called, cannot be
adequately clarified and accurately understood without
a reappraisal of the factors that have moulded its identity.

It was in the 1950s and 1960s that large numbers of
blacks from the Caribbean, including a significant
Christian fraternity, were recruited to fill numerous job
vacancies, mainly in the service industries of post-war
Britain. The majority of these people naturally wished
to preserve and uphold their profound commitment to

12

God and worship within 'mainstream' churches, within whose Caribbean branches more than fifty per cent were full members. While many encountered widespread rejection on racial grounds, others were alienated by the nominal tendencies of the British church, particularly those used to the more fundamentalist and spiritual emphasis characteristic of the Caribbean expression of faith.

Significantly, sociologists have maintained that black people have not really escaped slavery, and race alone consequently 'determines their social, economic and political position'.[1] It also seems true that race alone has determined our religious—or more particularly, Christian—status, especially in view of the kind of rejection Caribbean Christians faced in Britain. The rejection of those who ultimately became the pioneers of the so-called 'black-led' church was apparently based solely on their black skin, which relegated their faith to an inferior status. This sense of inferiority/superiority in religion in general, and in the Christian faith in particular, appears (for black Christians, at least) to have much to do with the sociological and racial value-judgements that are made by both secular society and the church.

The superiority myth

It is now well documented that Europeans in the seventeenth and eighteenth centuries were fed with pseudo-scientific and racist myths about black people in order to justify slavery. The most disturbing and effective of these included questions about identity: were black people really human? In his *History of Jamaica* (1774) Edward Long declared:

> . . . these acts they are libidinous and shameless as monkeys or baboons. The equally hot temperament of their women

has given probability to the charge of their admitting these animals frequently to their embrace . . . In general, negroes are void of genius and seem almost incapable of making progress in civility or science. . . . They are the vilest of humankind to which they have little more pretentions of resemblance than what arises from their exterior form.[2]

The same judgement is evident a century later in Charles Parham's comment about the 'disgusting Southern darkey camp meetings',[3] with which he disparagingly compared William Seymour's Azusa Street Revival of 1906. More recently, when Christians from the Caribbean attended 'mainstream' Churches in Britain, they were asked by clergy not to return as 'your presence will unsettle our parishioners'. This comment implied that blacks were some sort of sub-human being.

This superiority myth has been fostered and perpetuated by the privileged rulers; by administrators of education, employment and housing, who all too frequently passed inferior services and accommodation to black people. Their social, political, economic and religious status as determined by race alone has rooted black people in a distinct 'caste' in Britain. Their tenacious rejection of the nonentity status, however, has led many out of the social, economic and religious wilderness. It must be with equal determination, at least within the scope of this present work, that the true identity of these groups of Christians be properly and permanently established as a significant step towards full participation and recognition in the life of the British church.

Where groups of people such as Caribbeans are alienated, especially on religious grounds, the consequence is invariably that they accept their alienation and form their own communities of faith. David Shepherd gives clear assent to this principle, commenting, 'It is a natural reaction of a group which feels shut out from the mainstream life in a country to strengthen its own community life; it is natural for churches to be focus points of such a community, as black churches are today.'[4] Caribbean Christians, however, were not simply forming new communities of faith; they were already members of recognised denominations, forced to develop apart from the 'mainstream' churches in this strange land. But the need to continue worshipping God was not merely a reaction to the superiority myth; of course other factors affected the development and growth of Caribbean Christian groups in Britain and have characterised our worship. We'll look at some of these in the course of this chapter.

The image and likeness of God

It is within the constitution of the human race to worship God, and the Christian, black or white, is presumably at ease in his worship of the Triune God. Humanity's creation in the image and likeness of God (Gen 1:26–27) is a clear statement of its purpose. Human beings have also been given supremacy in the cosmos; and though we are an integral part of the natural order, we cannot find the true meaning and purpose for our existence in that context alone; our final destiny is not to be found in our dominion over the world, nor indeed in our power of reason, but ultimately in our positive response to God, through a personal relationship with him. This provides the framework within which we fully experience the true purpose of our existence. We were made to worship God, and that need must ultimately find fulfilment. Alienated Christians from the Caribbean, therefore, fulfilled an innate desire for worship by meeting in kitchens, bedrooms, living rooms, and, when numbers became too large, in school and church halls. Though they often encountered great reluctance from administrators and incumbent clergy when searching for this accommodation, it was from these vital, yet difficult and humble beginnings that the so-called 'black-led' church has come about. In view of these and other highly relevant considerations, the question of whether 'black-led' is an accurate and acceptable identification demands further investigation.

A new phenomenon

The phenomenon of the 'black-led' church has in the last thirty-five years been as staggering as its growth. Its pioneers were mainly simple but devout men and women who worshipped God with passion and sincerity. Such has been the rapidity of its growth during these years that 'The Growth of the Black-led Church in Britain' has become a much-used title for a multiplicity of discussions, essays, articles, books and other assorted papers in recent times, all seeking to understand and describe the nature of this brand of faith, and the factors affecting its increase and importance. It is interesting to note, however, that the growth rate of Afro-Caribbean churches between 1979 and 1989 was a mere four per cent.[5] Needless to say, it has not been with much prominence, except in a very few cases[6] that the 'black-led' church itself has been engaged in this task of describing the phenomenon. In fact the research has mainly been by whites, whose discourses ranged from the purely socio-economic to historical and theological papers. Much of this work, of course, has to be assessed on the basis of the researcher's primary objective. Roswith Gerloff,[7] for example, has to be credited for her perspective to enhance and promote unity between black and white people. Paul Charman's *Reflections,*

Black and White Christians in the City,[8] sought most boldly to foster greater understanding about black people and their relatively misunderstood brand of faith—and thereby the promotion of Christian unity.

In the meantime, the black-led church fought consistently for survival and recognition as a significant presence in Britain. This process was greatly assisted by its acquisition of freehold property and organisation of structures which have largely secured its future. It has established community care projects, ensuring that its elderly and children receive adequate care and education, and it is renowned for its high degree of free-spirited but largely orderly evangelical worship. The infectiousness of this mode of worship has been evident in other evangelical Christian groups, evident by their inclusion of musical instruments (including very 'noisy' drums), and hand-clapping in their heretofore 'quiet' style of worship.

The black-led church has now reached a watershed in its history; one that is noticeable in many respects. First, there is now a fresh desire to understand and describe the theological, historical and racio-cultural background of the black-led church; to face and question those traditions and theological nuances, as well as the misconceptions that have frequently been the cause of much unnecessary division and disunity. There has also been a new desire among black Christians to explain the positive social, moral and spiritual influences which brought cohesion, and contributed to their identity.

The identity described

An important aspect of this self-examination is the process by which identity has been conferred on these church groups by researchers and social scientists. Labels such as 'black', 'Pentecostal', 'black-led', and 'West Indian' are part of a vocabulary variously used to describe local churches in England whose leadership and membership are predominantly West Indian in origin. Only within the past twenty years have these terms come into the relevant literature, especially from the mid- to late-1970s, and more recently by the Community Religious Project of the Department of Theology and Religious Studies at Leeds University. In this project, Vanessa Howard defined the term 'black-led', for example, as those churches 'which have black leadership and where membership is predominantly black'.[9] A number of research projects have since been published and the term 'black-led' is invariably favoured. In their work, both Roswith Gerloff and Paul Charman consistently use it throughout. In all examples of its use, this phrase has to all intents and purposes been *imposed* on the Christian community by researchers who sought to understand and describe. It is important from a black perspective, therefore, to discover to what extent these terms—'black-led' in particular—have correctly described our Christian community. Even if only briefly, we need to look at some biological and sociological implications of the words used, and at their impact on the religious and cultural identity of black people in Britain. We can thus reach a better understanding of worship within our denominations.

Heritage and baggage

In one most notable respect the term 'black', used as a prefix or standing alone, cannot be challenged or questioned as to its appropriateness: it describes people born with black skins. (This is true even if some Asians, who share the racial discrimination, also appropriate the term.) This unchangeable fact of course means that the whole race cannot change its skin pigmentation; it is the 'natural colouring' of that race. Given this undeniable circumstance, researchers were correct to reflect the colour in their terminology, though as we shall discover 'black' may not be satisfactorily used in the description of all these church groups.

A second observation is crucial. Since a person's blackness is irreversible, and since black people, it must be assumed, are completely content with their biological and created heritage (God said: 'Let us make man in our image, after our likeness,' Gen 1:26–27, which includes all humanity), there is no logical or ethical reason for black people to try to justify our heritage by using defensive or polemic language given to us by others in an attempt to define our religious experience.

The demolition of racial barriers is quite clearly stated in St Paul's reflection on the specific purpose of the Incarnation and Resurrection when he said: 'There is neither Jew nor Greek, there is neither slave nor free man, there is neither male nor female; for you are all one in Christ Jesus' (Gal 3:28, NASB). Christians have all entered into the unity of the body of Christ and ought to express that unity by the variety of gifts given to each. Together, these facts tend to make any distinction drawn on the basis of Christian religious or biological considerations completely unnecessary, as it must do on racial grounds.

Not everyone, however, is discontent with the term 'black' in this particular context. Iain MacRobert[10] regards it as indicative of a mode of worship characterised by rhythms and forms peculiar to African culture and heritage, which, of course, have been reflected in the American, Caribbean, and now British black Christian life and worship, and which constitute an essential aspect of our identity.

Even so, an assessment of the sociological implications of the term 'black' reveals the destructive and painful connotations all too often associated with 'blackness'. 'Black Friday', 'Black Monday', the 'black sheep of the family', and the general reflection of unhelpful or bad conditions like the 'black-list', 'black-mail'—all these convey ideas of wickedness and gloom. Such associations affect the way in which things and people are perceived, and help to mould the beliefs and values of the perceiver. At the same time, infinitely more dangerous pseudo-scientific myths perpetuated during the eighteenth and nineteenth centuries have led to many discriminatory and racist attitudes against black people. Many of these are still current in a subtle but powerful way. Not only have these associations, myths and misconceptions informed individual attitudes, but they have also affected the policies of governments and institutions in the modern world, obviously loaded heavily against the black person.

Bishop David Shepherd fully acknowledged this fact when he cited Lord Simey's speech of 1966 in the House of Lords:

> . . . our coloured fellow-citizens . . . had been educated in our schools, spoke our common language . . . but because of their colour they were given unskilled jobs . . . the first to become unemployed in a slump, they had the worst accommodation, the worst social services and the worst neighbourhood to live in . . . May God help us if we lose equality of citizenship with people merely because they are coloured.[11]

The situation of 1966 pertains today, not only to

Liverpool, of which Shepherd wrote, but to much of the rest of Britain and the Western world. 'The confinement of negroes to the lowest stratum is clearly a national condition,' says Leonard Reissman. 'Because of race alone the negro has been kept in the bottom economic class, in the bottom status group and in the most ineffectual power position.'[12]

These conditions have even led governments to legislate against black people, as in the South African apartheid state. Furthermore, whites have not only imposed this secondary or marginalised social status as chief controllers of economic and political power (for reasons too detailed to reflect here), but have created significant tension in the mind of the black person about his own identity; such white people are therefore less than qualified to determine that identity, as in the term 'black-led'. It would be complacent and wrong if this imposed identity were regarded as sacred and accurately reflective of the experience and ecclesiology of black Christians in Britain.

The important place our church has come to assume in a multi-racial, multi-denominational evangelical structure is evident, in particular, by the wide usage of the term 'black-led'. It becomes vital, therefore, for an accurate understanding of the growth, theology and ecclesiology of this branch of evangelical Christianity, and for its identity to be comprehensive and true, not only for white researchers alone, but also for black adherents. I turn now to consider specifically the other principal terms that are frequently used.

'The black church'

The first and most obvious term in use is 'black church'. This has encountered much resistance and repulsion

because of its separatist and discriminatory overtones
against other races. While the ethnic make-up of these
churches is predominantly (and in some cases exclusively) black, few, if any, would consciously discourage
or discriminate against members of other racial groups.
Use of the term 'black church' naturally invites criticism
of this kind, and given that the term necessarily justifies
the ethnic origin of the majority of its members in
Britain, its heritage is rooted in the Incarnation and
Resurrection of Jesus Christ, the precise source of
salvation for whites and all others. On the other hand,
'black church', it may be argued, reaffirms the racial
identity of its black adherents, and also asserts a peculiar social and moral cohesiveness that has been the
inevitable result of being 'black' (and rejected) in a white
society. The 'black church' has also come to be indicative of a religio-cultural tradition that is characteris-
tically 'missionary' and 'Caribbean' in expression,
and unhelpfully tends to preclude from its life those
would-be black adherents born in Britain.

Much of the Christian influence and teaching in the
Caribbean—the springboard for the 'black church' in
Britain today—has been attributable to Southern white
American missionaries. The main thrust of this missionary message was holiness as an invisible and inward
work, and which visibly manifests itself outwardly in
language, dress and social habits. Though the early
teaching was less of the European doctrinal expository
type, these Protestant missionaries started with the
death, atonement and resurrection of Christ, together
with eternal life for those committed to him. More
particularly, many white missionaries constantly stressed
the *outward* expression, often to the neglect of good
biblical exegesis on the decisive *inward* work. For

instance, in the 1860 General Conference of the Wesleyan Methodist Church (now the Wesleyan Holiness Church), it was stipulated that commitment to modest dress, no visits to places of amusement, no divorce or remarriage, no jewellery, limited recreation and no tobacco—described as 'a great evil and unbecoming to a Christian, a waste of the Lord's money, and a defilement of the body'—was necessary for conversion. Some in the Pilgrim Holiness movement, which also emphasised abstinence from these things, went further in the General Assembly in 1938, when an unsuccessful proposal to ban the wedding ring was made. Its General Conference of 1955 voted it unconstitutional to receive a person into membership until he stopped wearing gold.

This disposition towards stress on the outward appearance (mainly of female members) as a vital mark of holiness prevails also within the Church of God of Prophecy and the New Testament Church of God; but these issues were common in their application and acceptance among Caribbean Christians as a whole. In addition many slaves and their descendants were taught to read from the Lord's Prayer and the Decalogue in the King James version of the Bible, hence a revered and almost inviolable appreciation of that version by many Christians, and a mode of speech in the very elderly which occasionally betrays the nature of their early education.

All these factors have influenced what has come to be called the 'black church', and while good ethics, high moral standards and modesty all have their authority in Scripture, the cultural baggage attracted and reinforced by this particular missionary emphasis has not always reflected the best course in Christian expression. In the

colonial Caribbean, it has seriously restricted the education and training of the masses of eventual emigrants,
out of whom many leaders and pastors emerged to
pioneer and guide the church in Britain. The present
leadership is largely of that generation of very devout
early immigrants—many of them the 'fruit' of the efforts
of those Holiness Movement white missionaries.

In addition, congregations referred to as the 'black
church' are not exclusively comprised of black people.
A number of the established denominations in Britain
have white leadership at their American headquarters,
for example, the Wesleyan Holiness Church, the New
Testament Church of God and the Church of God of
Prophecy. Furthermore, a number of our churches have
a few white members in Britain and white pastors in the
USA. In this context, 'black church' refers specifically to
the British experience, and recognition of two factors
becomes important. First, it would be somewhat arro-
gant, to say the least, and certainly unscriptural, to
ignore white membership in Britain regardless of the
small numbers involved; and secondly, white people
should be given every encouragement to become members of any denomination in the true biblical fashion
of the unified church. Consequently, the descriptive
wording that includes 'black' could work against the
church's mandate to evangelise *all* people.

In spite of everything, a proportion of black Christians
within black-led churches would still affirm the use of
'black church', since by its use they are not only
affirming their racial identity, but also some degree of
pride in being black—even if only in reaction to white
prejudice. On the other hand, many black Christians
born in Britain would understandably prefer to disclaim
the cultural identity that is in many cases distinctly

Caribbean, if only because they have no first-hand knowledge or experience of it, especially of those elements interwoven with the prevailing conception of biblical holiness. While these second and third generation Caribbean descendants would also affirm and be proud of their *biological* and *cultural* identity, the idea of a 'black church' does not become an easy option for them.

'The black-led church'; the 'Pentecostal' church

The most frequently used of the imposed terminology is 'black-led church'. This descriptive label was first used in the early 1970s research done by Roswith Gerloff.[13] It is infinitely more accurate and respectable, however, than the term 'sect', used by Malcolm J.C. Calley, who explains:

> By 'sects' I understand a religious group, within a more general religious tradition, which recruits by voluntary association ... A 'church' on the other hand, does not depend on converts for the bulk of its members, but recruits naturally, the children of members becoming members as they grow up.[14]

True, Calley's research was done in the early stages of the development of these churches in Britain, and he could not be expected to have the benefit of hindsight of their growth today. To describe them as 'sects', however, he seemed to have ignored the fact that what largely differentiated them from their original Christian tradition was their transplantation in England via immigration rather than evangelisation. These groups, moreover, were formed into denominations well before their establishment in England.

It has already been noted that some regard 'black-led' as a politically emotive phrase with racial overtones. While its use aims to emphasise positively that the

leadership is given by those mainly distinguished by
ethnic origin, not all churches with predominantly black
congregations are in fact 'black-led'. Some 'mainstream'
churches in Britain with black communicants engage
black ministers, but these are not necessarily 'black-led'
since their internal leadership is white. Even so,
the cardinal doctrines of God and salvation are not
expressed in a fundamentally different way from that of
the 'black-led' church, except for the difference of the
'Oneness'[15] emphasis in some. Furthermore, some
churches with black congregations in the USA have
white ministers, but largely black and white leadership
in the UK, such as the United Pentecostal Church. The
term 'black-led' is also thought by some black ministers
to be deeply offensive; Malachi Ramsay has remarked
that it is 'degrading and lacking in respect';[16] his is by
no means an isolated view. The church whose members
and British leaders are predominantly black may now
wish to identify itself according to these historical and
theological foundations, but also on the basis of its
experience; it must avoid descriptions, however, that
perpetuate the social, political, economic and cultural-
religious negatives that resound in the term 'black-led'.
This term may imply independence from its American
leadership. But for the church in Britain to seek full
independence from its white American headquarters
simply to justify the 'black-led' label is a foolish attempt
to emphasise its racial heritage, which is anyway God-
given. In any case, this phrase would not change the
exclusivist and separatist connotations that work not
only against its Christian identity, but also restrict the
biblical concepts of mission and unity of the body,
regardless of ethnic origin (Acts 15:1–11).

Again, these churches are frequently referred to as

'black-led Pentecostal' churches, or 'West Indian Pentecostalism', or simply 'the Pentecostal church'. Here 'Pentecostal' and 'black' are used synonymously; but a number of difficulties arise here. To begin with, there are obvious examples of churches whose ministers and congregations are black, but not necessarily 'Pentecostal'. The Bibleway Church and Wesleyan Holiness Church are cases in point. The latter church's doctrinal position is fundamentally Methodist, though its style of worship may be quite similar to that of most Pentecostal churches. It is in the theology of the spiritual gifts that some difference is evident—the gift of tongues in particular. It is true, however, to say that the majority of churches whose congregations and pastors are mainly black are 'Pentecostal', with variations in style and theological emphasis. For 'Pentecostalism' in all of these terms is primarily distinguished by its regard for speaking in tongues as the initial evidence of baptism in the Holy Spirit, and as a work subsequent to conversion.

It would be much more precise if these churches were named according to their historical and theological foundations. The Holiness revivals of mid- to late-nineteenth-century America gave birth to the majority of them, and while doctrinal emphasis changed, the cardinal beliefs have not varied. The doctrine of entire sanctification, for example, does not differ fundamentally from 'baptism with the Holy Spirit'—a subject too detailed to be dealt with here. It is sufficient merely to acknowledge that while many churches have the distinctiveness of being 'Pentecostal', the same churches are also happy to stress the necessity and importance of all spiritual gifts, and would not regard tongues as fundamental for faith, redemption, or future salvation, in the same way that they are constrained to accept the need for preaching, conversion and baptism by immersion.

The words 'West Indian' or 'Afro-Caribbean' Church are also occasionally used. All the foregoing observations about cultural identity and evangelistic restriction equally apply here, and the need of the increasing numbers of second and third generation descendants of this ethnic group cannot be ignored. Any treatise on worship within these churches of mainly Caribbean people has to recognise that while many of these Christian groups have either purchased their own buildings or are sharing with another denomination, designations like 'West Indian' or 'Afro-Caribbean' are inadequate. Any original suitability in them has diminished as the church has developed.

The possibility of an adequate terminology?

The difficulties in the current terms cannot be over-stated, but it seems equally problematic to construct an all-embracing and accurate description, especially given the large number of different denominations which have developed over the last thirty years. Indeed, is a label necessary at all now that these denominations have properly established themselves in Britain, sharing a common identity with others in Christ?

What is essential is that if there must be a descriptive term that identifies our churches for religious and cultural purposes, it will need to reflect that potentially enriching diversity, at least in the ethnic composition of the congregations, while at the same time contributing to the unity that all Christians share (see 1 Cor 12:4–27; Eph 2:11–22). The body of Christ has not been caste in colour, class or creed, but the Word was made flesh for all, and racial barriers were broken down in the Crucifixion and Resurrection.

Identification in the mainstream churches

The 'mainstream' denominations (Anglicans, Catholics, Baptists, URC and Methodists) are identified primarily by theology and church tradition. Anglicanism, for example, is an episcopal system, with a nationalistic title ('Church of England'). In the New Testament the Greek word *episcopos* means 'bishop' or 'overseer' and is applied pre-eminently to Christ (1 Pet 2:25), and then to leaders of local congregations (Phil 1:1). This term was used as a generic description of the office, its meaning defined in accordance with the qualifications demanded by the church (see 1 Tim 3:1ff; Tit 1:7). There appears to be little indication in Scripture of the rule of a single bishop, but the early church defenders Ignatius of Antioch and Ireneaus of Lyons[17] were the first to insist on a monarchical episcopacy—a system of one bishop over all other bishops. Scripture and the tradition of the church Fathers, therefore, seems central to the process of identification of this church, as well as the Roman Catholic Church.

The Baptist Church is identified by the theological position that defends adult baptism as the apostolic method of admitting members to church fellowship. The Methodist Church is so called because of a nickname attached to John Wesley and his colleagues at Oxford University who prayed, read Scripture and studied 'methodically'. Methodism was founded, however, on the biblical doctrine of justification by faith through grace, and stressed sanctification based on the exegesis of texts such as 1 Thessalonians 5:23.

Greek orthodoxy is so called not so much because of

its doctrinal position, but because of the tradition.[18]
The term 'orthodoxy' in Greek simply means 'the right
opinion'. In Eastern Orthodoxy, however, 'classical
tradition' developed through creeds and councils by the
early church Fathers as a defence of the Church against
heresy lies at the heart of its identity.

Clearly, then, the identification of the 'mainstream'
church has emerged primarily from biblical interpretation built on analytical expositions of Scripture, or a
defence of biblical faith, not by race or colour as in the
term 'black-led'. (Quite noticeable, however, is the
development of 'house churches', whose growth between 1979 and 1989 reached 144 per cent,[19] and who
seem to have avoided the problem of a suitable name.)

The Holiness Movement

We have seen that the common theological root of
the so-called 'black-led' church is in the Holiness
Movement. This movement emphasised biblical holiness
as separation *from* self *to* God. The Greek term *hagios*
(holy) has a very strong sense of 'separation from'
common use, and 'consecration to' a hallowed state (1
Thess 3:13; 2 Cor 7:1). The movement began in nineteenth-century America when Methodism had lost its
emphasis on the Bible and sanctification, and it sought
to restore power to Christianity through a re-emphasis
of these in the revivalist camp meetings, mainly in the
southern USA and in parts of New York State and the
Midwest. Sanctification and speaking in tongues were
considered by Wesley as signs of baptism with the Holy
Spirit; he had also made a distinction between both of
these and the state of the ordinary Christian.

The Holiness Movement also stressed freedom from
'carnal-mindedness'—for example, gambling, smoking

tobacco, alcohol, swearing, adultery and social dancing—and emphasised 'outward holiness'. In addition,
female decorum merited special attention: the body
being fully clothed by dresses with full or elbow-length
sleeves, hems below the knees, and no low necks;
covered heads, understood by many as the wearing of
hats in worship (some women will not now enter a
church without a hat or scarf on their heads); unplaited
hair (understood as non-straightened hair). But Holiness
theology was essentially a combination of Methodism
and the doctrine of Christian perfection, and it differed
from 'fundamentalism' in that it was more oriented to
ethics and spiritual life than to the defence of doctrinal
orthodoxy. The Pentecostal and Holiness Churches
emerged from these waves of revival, becoming separated only on the issues of tongues and organisational
structures.

Another concern is the distinction to be made between culture (in Caribbean terms) and Christianity,
though of course these are not mutually exclusive. The
churches in question have the very special problem of a
difficult mixture of 'American-Caribbean' culture with
a strong African content on one hand (ladies' dress
codes, language, innate rhythms, the unwritten liturgy,
etc), and on the other a different attitude from those
born in Britain to the same cultural elements, which
would be ignored to the church's peril. Yet, to address
this situation adequately may entail abandoning use of
the term 'Holiness' with its connotation of spiritual
superiority, since this use of it would at best be artificial
and at worst unscriptural.

'Holiness Church' would not call attention to race as
'black-led' does, since there is no implication of ethni-
city in the term; nor would it imply any organisational

structure based on a race. Churches with white leadership in the USA and an almost exclusively black leadership in Britain, if the British churches were brought by independence or greater participation of talented and able black leaders to equality at all levels of leadership and administration, would not be affected either doctrinally or historically by the duality, for example, of the names 'Holiness Church' (British) and the Church of God or Wesleyan Church (American).

New labels reflecting the theological reasons why our churches came into existence would eliminate the inaccuracies inherent in the terms 'Afro-Caribbean', 'Caribbean', 'West Indian', 'Pentecostal', 'black' or 'black-led' churches, but not at the expense of racial, religious or cultural identity, black or white. The Caribbean cultural elements would, with appropriate biblical studies, be identified and separated as voluntary or incidental, not essential to the biblical requirements for faith.

But the implications of omitting or subsuming 'Pentecostal' cannot easily be ignored. First, there is a long scriptural tradition attached to this title, and the idea of omitting it would only be accepted with great difficulty; second, the theological differences (tongues, foot-washing) associated with it may be blurred, at least in principle; and third, the instant connotations of the word 'Pentecostal' (indicating passionate and open worship with an unwritten liturgy) could disappear. But if the term 'Pentecostal' *were* dropped, the biblical ideals of cross-cultural evangelism and multi-racial fellowship could be better served, in addition to immediate identification of our churches with the wider evangelical tradition in Britain. The church, black, white or mixed, must offer a new mode of life to *all* people; and that alternative is found only in its message of salvation by faith through grace available to all in Christ.

The phrase 'Holiness-Pentecostal Church', already in use by some writers, would, of course, provide an accurate alternative, because of the 'Holiness' origin and the 'Pentecostal' distinctiveness, even if the latter has its foundation in the former. Yet some Pentecostal movements (white churches) that do not immediately connote 'Pentecostalism' (as popularly understood), may lie outside this term and invite even greater confusion.

It is not too difficult to see the need for an all-embracing term of identification that would satisfy diversity, ecclesiology and theology, culture and spirituality in the kingdom of God. It seems clear that a non-nationalistic or non-racial title may be used with great effectiveness.

While this discussion seeks to raise the appropriate questions and to stimulate dialogue on this important issue, it is clear that there are no simple answers. What seems to be a highly attractive approach is the use of a name that identifies our churches both theologically and historically. This would necessarily involve some combination of the 'Holiness' and 'Pentecostal' labels.

It is within the context of this reappraisal and analysis of the imposed 'black-led' title that worship within churches of mainly black adherents originating or descending from the Caribbean can be best understood, since clarification of the peculiar features of our church community will contribute to an enlightened understanding of our worship, and advance the permanent establishment of the church's true identity.

Notes

1. Smelser, Neil J., *Sociology, An Introduction* (New York, 1967), p 241.
2. Ward, Tim, 'Growth of the Black-led Churches in Britain' (unpublished article).
3. Synan, Vinson, *The Holiness-Pentecostal Movement in the United States* (Eerdmans: Grand Rapids, 1971), p 180.
4. Shepherd, David, *Bias to the Poor* (London, 1985) p 00.
5. Marc Europe, *English Churches Census* (1991).
6. Works by black Christians include Ira Brooks' *Another Gentleman to the Ministry* (Compeer Press, Birmingham); *Building Bridges* (Hodder: 1988), by Philip Mohabir; and *Conversations with Five Black Pastors: Catching Both Sides of the Wind* (British Council of Churches, 1985), by Anita Jackson.
7. Gerloff, Roswith, *Partnership between Black and White* (Methodist Home Mission, 1977).
8. Charman, Paul, *Reflections, Black and White Christians in the City* (Zebra Project: London, 1979).
9. Howard, Venessa, *A Report on Afro-Caribbean Christianity in Britain* (Community Religious Project, Leeds University, 1987).
10. MacRobert, Iain, Lecture sponsored by ACEA's Youth Network, Birmingham, 1991.
11. Shepherd, David, *Op Cit*, p 33.
12. Smelser, Neil J., *Op Cit*, p 240.
13. Gerloff, Roswith, *Op Cit*.
14. Calley, Malcolm J.C., *God's People, West Indian Pentecostal Sects in England* (London, 1965), p 2.
15. 'Oneness' is a non-Trinitarian theological position that stresses singularity in the Godhead, eg, baptism 'in the name of Jesus' only, rather than 'in the name of the Father and of the Son and of the Holy Spirit'.
16. *Faith in the City*, A Report of the Archbishop of Canterbury's Commission on Urban Priority Areas (London, 1986), p 42.

17. Walker, Williston, *A History of the Christian Church* (T&T Clark: Edinburgh, 1976), pp 41–42.

18. Braaten, Carl E., (ed), *Perspectives on Nineteenth and Twentieth Century Protestant Theology* (SCM: London, 1967), p 9.

19. Marc Europe, *Op Cit.*

2

Biblical Worship

Ronald Nathan

'. . . there was an Ethiopian . . . and he had come to Jerusalem to worship' (Acts 8:27 NASB).

The parameters of any study on biblical worship are established by the Bible, the self-revelation of God. This revelation was shaped in varied cultures and presented to us within the background of several countries, since it was written over a period of 1,400 years and by at least forty different writers.

It is of paramount importance to note that the Bible does not actually seek to define the term 'worship'. Instead, it provides a basis for worship and presupposes that mankind needs to worship. It also enables worship to be wholesome in its expression. General principles of worship are found in its records of epics, prophecies and historical accounts.

Definitions of worship

The Oxford Dictionary defines worship as 'to honour and revere a supernatural being, to adore with appropriate acts, rites and ceremonies'. The New Bible Dictionary[1] states that the essential concept of worship in both the Old and the New Testaments is *service*. The Hebrew word used to denote worship is *aboda*, a word whose root is drawn from the labour of slaves and hired servants and which carries the overtones of service specifically to Jehovah.

Israel's worship was focused on the God of Abraham, Isaac and Jacob. Their faith was monotheistic (a belief in one God) and could not therefore accommodate the worship of any other deity. This principle was enshrined in the Hebrew law 'Thou shalt worship no other god' (Ex 34:14). Judgement was instantaneous for the disobedient (Deut 8:19; 11:16–17; 30:17–18).

In the New Testament several Greek words are used to refer to worship. The most frequent of these are: *proskuneo*, *sebamai*, *sebazomai*, *latrueo*, *eusebeo*, and *therapueo*. The Greek word *proskuneo* is used widely in the Gospels, Acts and the Apocrypha. Only once is it used in the Pauline epistles (1 Cor 14:25), and its original meaning stems from two Greek words *pros* (towards) and *kuneo* (to kiss). *Proskuneo* thus expresses the idea of kissing the hand in homage; to make obeisance or to bow down in surrender.

Sebamai and *sebazomai* concentrate on the underlying attitude of reverence, to feelings of awe and devotion. The emphasis is placed on the overriding presence of God in our midst.

Latrueo is used in a similar way to *proskuneo*, to give homage, but with the added emphasis of service intrinsic in its usage (see Phil 3:3).

Eusebeo links worship to pious acts. In Acts 17:23 Paul uses it in relation to the Athenians' objects of worship. This word takes in the element of ritualistic observance.

Therapueo denotes the healing process that worship engenders. Worship and healing come together through a washing of our being as we approach God. This word throws light on the fact that the Jewish priesthood went

through several ceremonial washings before coming to
God.

Even as we praise, healing properties are released into
us, body and soul. Our vision expands, our inner beings
are strengthened, and our spirits are liberated to
worship beyond earthly limitations.

The object of worship

The Hebrews worshipped Yahweh, the Creator, who
sought a special relationship with his people. He
declared openly that he is a jealous God, righteous
and just, yet merciful and loving; all-powerful, all-
knowing and omnipresent; sovereign over the affairs of
mankind yet approachable by many different means.
God has put within mankind the need to worship him
as a personal God, to know him who desires the
worship of his people and inhabits the praise of his
people.

Principles of worship

Essential to the worship of the Hebrews was the altar,
an elevated area upon which the sacrifice was made,
either accepted or rejected. It was here that the worshipper gained approval or disapproval. Further action
was very much dependent on this simple but vital
ceremony. And because it was at the core of Old
Testament religious practice, the importance of the altar
cannot be over-emphasised.

There was at first a great degree of flexibility about
the type of construction and the sites of a Hebrew altar.
Later with the Tabernacle and the Temple, a more
clearly defined form of worship developed. Even with

its elaborate vestures and outward ceremonial para-
phernalia, the Lord also expected the sacrifice of an
inward and heart-felt remorse for sins committed
against him, and a willingness to repent. Samuel the
prophet declared 'to obey is better than sacrifice' (1 Sam
15:22). This changing emphasis removed the notion
that some sort of magical properties were inherent in
the altar, a view popular in the surrounding nations of
that time.

The New Bible Commentary[2] points out 'that the Old
Testament chronicler of the period of the Books of
Kings and Chronicles sees the cult with its worship of
God's feasts, priests and singers as the underlying
support of Israel's existence'. It is thus extremely difficult to divorce worship from sacrifice and sacrifice
from service. In Scripture they are two dimensions of the
same thing. Later in Israelite history, the prophet Micah
proclaimed, 'He has shewed thee, O man, what is good;
and what doth the Lord require of thee but to do justly,
and to love mercy, and to walk humbly with thy God'
(Mic 6:8). Herein lies worship and its interrelations
between God and man: a lifestyle pleasing to God and
committed to the development of others. If this overriding principle is lost, every aspect of worship is devoid
of meaning and social impact.

Over twelve feasts are mentioned in the Old Testament.
The impact of these feasts, festivals and sacred holy days
cannot and must not be overlooked in any analysis of
worship. These impressed upon the common folk the
acts of God in their daily lives. On these special
occasions, the teachings of Yahweh are embodied and
illustrated with dramatic effects and symbols. This style
of worship would pass on to the populace information
about the required practices of Israel in its relationship

to Yahweh. Worship was not just a product of the 'professionals' (priests, prophets or kings), for the people would share in the proclamation of the faith.

When we come to the New Testament, this rich Jewish tradition plays a major role in shaping the fabric of the early church's worship. Jesus here reiterates that God alone is to be worshipped (Mk 12:28–31 and 22:33–39). When he enters into discourse with the Samaritan woman (Jn 4:42), we are able to draw out several principles for worship. The conversation between them took place in the city of Sychar, in Samaria. According to the Jews, this was unholy ground; they had no dealings with the Samaritans (Jn 4:9), and there was a hot debate at the time about whether one place was holier than another (ie, Jerusalem or Mount Gerazim). Jesus' response to this debate was to give priority to the life-giving quality of eternal water rather than the veneration of patriarch or sacred site (Jn 4:9–14). God is interested in the heart, and Jesus points the woman towards the way of worship rather than the site. He also points out to the woman that worship cannot be entered into amid ignorance of the truth; this is especially so in relation to the nature of God. As he told the Samaritan woman then, God is Spirit, and they who worship him must worship him in spirit and in truth (Jn 4:24).

Worship transcends the spiritual, psychological, mental and physical dimensions of mankind (Mt 22:36–39). Writing to the Romans, Paul expounds on these dimensions when he suggests (12:1–3) that we ought to worship the Lord with all of our lives.

> Therefore, I urge you, brothers, in view of God's mercy, to offer your bodies as living sacrifices, holy and pleasing to God—which is your spiritual worship. Do not conform

any longer to the pattern of this world, but be transformed by the renewing of your mind. Then you will be able to test and approve what God's will is—his good, pleasing and perfect will.

Here Paul uses the term *parakaleo* (beseech, implore, beg) to alert the church that what follows represents God's deep desire for the believer. The appeal is made on the basis of what God has done for the church through Christ and his atoning sacrifice (Rom 4–11). Paul makes it clear that God's deep desire is for the believer to offer his *whole* body or being to God. With this complete self-giving follow transformation, renewal and fulfilment. This self-offering must be in a conscious, intelligent and consecrated devotion to God. Our lifestyles are to be transformed on a day-by-day basis.

Scripture also teaches that this worship, honouring God in all things, should not be limited to a few hours on a Sunday. Believers should worship God through their daily life experiences: eating, work, family matters, personal relations, ownership of property, etc. Only worshipping and worshipful people will make up a worshipping and worshipful community of believers.

These views of worship are foundational to any adequate analysis of it both today and in the days of the New and Old Testaments. As Calvin Coolidge said, 'It is only when men begin to worship that they begin to grow.'

Elements of worship

In both the Old and New Testament worship a variety of elements is intrinsic. Whereas some of the Old Testament festivals, ceremonies and rites were similar to those of the surrounding nations (eg, circumcision) others were peculiar to Israel (eg, Passover). In New Testament days some of these practices were part of the legacy inherited from the Old Testament (eg, the liturgical styles from Temple worship). In such cases the old elements of worship were imbued with new vitality and meaning as people grew in the knowledge of their God and their experience of the Holy Spirit.

Prayer

Prayer of course plays a pivotal role in worship. If worship embraces all the attitudes and emotional experiences of the human spirit, prayer stimulates submission, humility, adoration, confession, supplication and thanksgiving:

> Prayer is the preface to the book of Christian living, the text of the new life sermon, the girding on the armour for battle, the pilgrim's preparation for his journey; and it must be supplemented by action or it amounts to nothing.[3]

Meditation on God's word results in a broken and contrite spirit. There can be no true reflection on God without penitence. This is one of the lessons we learn from the Old Testament prophets: the closer they drew to God, the more they were forced by the sheer brilliance of his holiness to fall upon their faces. Unlike today, prayer was then not seen as the manipulation of God, but as the alignment of our wills with his.

In the Old and New Testaments prayer is frequently mentioned and exercised, as there can be no doubt from the regularity of the use of the words 'pray' and 'prayer' (427 times). Spiritual maturity was evidenced on the practice of prayer. The apostles took note from Jesus that prayer was part and parcel of his lifestyle. When other important issues demanded the time given to prayer, they refused to be diverted from such a critical spiritual discipline (see Acts 6:4). Within the Pentecostal and charismatic movements there has been an emphasis on prayer.

Praise

Praise differs from prayer in that it seeks to underline the joy of being in a relationship with God. Praise is the expression of admiration, the ascribing of glory, as an act of worship. The psalmist lets us know that all human inventions, instruments—his whole being—can be put into the praise of God (Ps 150). He gives a panoramic view of the heights to which praise can go. Praise takes the individual out of the narrow confines of his selfishness to see the world at large as God determines.

Several aspects of praise are illustrated in the original languages of the Scriptures. Several Hebrew words for praise are used in the Old Testament, and each reveals the differing faces of praise. *Halal* expresses shouts of joy, jubilation and ecstatic utterances. *Yada* stresses praise through 'bodily actions', in dance, for example. *Zamar* highlights praise in music, as in singing or the playing of musical instruments. Similarly, in the New Testament, the Greek portrays praise as *eucharisten* (giving thanks), and *eulogein* (to bless).

Scripture reading and exposition

We have seen that out of the reading and exposition of Scripture the *scope* for worship is given, the *motivation* for worship is explained, the *parameters* of worship are established, and the *act* of worship is implored. On many occasions the Scriptures themselves prove to be a launching pad for worship. The preacher can create an atmosphere conducive to worship; good exegetical preaching of the word of God leads the congregation to worship; revelation of and meditation on the truth makes us submit ourselves in worship of God. It is no surprise then that the time given to the reading and preaching of the word in church is central to the order of service.

The results of worship

All who would accept God's rule over their lives, whatever their race, heritage, ability and status, become worshippers. Biblical worship is active, not passive. Since it lifts the person's entire being, it is holistic. The worshipper may laugh, cry, stand still, or shake; worship thus lends itself to extemporaneous expressions and ecstatic utterances. Its liturgy can be informative and systematic without losing touch with the realities of the worshippers' lives.

Worship easily incorporates the dramatic and the ritualistic, the spontaneous and the traditional. Various postures (kneeling, standing, uplifted hands, gesticulations, shouting, crying, clapping, etc) are all expressions of adoration and praise. Dance and drama also embody worship, letting it be expressed through the cultural fabric of the worshipper.

But we do not worship in isolation. Corporate worship is significant for the Christian today because it drives us away from the debilitating influence of Western individualism. When a group of believers meets in worship, their spirits are lifted up and exposed to God's word in an environment of communal adoration that draws them closer to each other and to God through Christ.

The innovative and creative potential of worship transformed the Catacombs into tabernacles in early days; today, third-world shacks become cathedrals. Slave plantations were converted into choir lofts for the production of now-familiar negro spirituals. Biblical worship is potent and explosive, for it arms individuals and the church with a sense both of the spiritual for eternity and the practical for the present. It restores self-respect: a network of relationships develops; group support is reinforced; the testimony, song or prayer illuminates the darkness—and the worshipper meets God.

Notes

1. InterVarsity Press. Leicester, 1982.
2. InterVarsity Press. Leicester, 1970.
3. Anonymous, from *Great Quotes and Illustrations* by George Sweeting.

3

The Pulpit Response to Worship
Joel Edwards

At the centre of black church worship is the declaration of the word of God. Preaching has always been the primary means by which the gospel has been made known. Paul's letter to Rome made the point: people cannot hear the Good News 'without a preacher' (Rom 10:14). Moreover, it is by faithful and consistent preaching that the worshipping community is sustained (2 Tim 4:2). In many ways the preacher stands as the catalyst of the praising event. Consequently, the pulpit occupies the central ground of the church's liturgical life by both *shaping* and *maintaining* the worship within the denominational setting. The minister is in fact the local worship leader.

The black preacher in context

In the black church, this central position of preaching is often greatly enhanced by the importance given to charismatic leadership and pastoral presence. Even if they are not able to discern spirits, black pastors are expected to be spiritually discerning! The congregation looks to the pulpit for guidance through the rapids of the spiritual torrents which sometimes produce excessive and unhelpful behaviour. They must provide the impetus in instances when a congregation evidently falls into spiritual slumber and ceases to be a worshipping community. What the trumpet is to the troops, the black pastor is to the congregation; he sounds the alarm, signals to battle or summons to praise.

The pastor's pivotal role in the church is the story of ordinary men and women repudiated by the world but elevated by the church. The stones rejected by the architects of society have become the cornerstones in the community of faith.

The privilege of the pulpit brings its own responsibilities and liabilities. Whether or not we wish to admit it, leadership intrinsically involves elements of authority and power. Sadly, our understanding of authority and power is frequently drawn from secular and political models rather than from the biblical idea of the suffering servant. A pastor who develops a personal power-base in the pulpit is unlikely to encourage true worship in the people. Dogmatic leadership, insensitive to the diversity of personal needs, may produce carbon copies of the pastor but it guarantees no mature worshippers.

The supreme duty of the minister is to make disciples and to lead people into the worship of God. If the minister is to generate true worship in the local church, he must act as a signpost to God rather than a symbol of God. The greatest becomes the least; the master becomes the slave; the preacher decreases, and Christ becomes enlarged in the hearts of the worshipping people. That is the joy of the minister. In the New Testament Paul refused to accept worship (Acts 14:13–15); Peter diverted it towards God (Acts 10:25, 26)—and the Christian leader must do the same. Power and authority must never be attributed to personal skills or acquired experience. Skills and abilities allow us to exert our *influence* in the local church and the community, but power is the work of the Holy Spirit leading us in the worship of the Saviour. In the pulpit power comes from God to enable us to serve effectively.

Respect

A distinct characteristic of the black church is the respect given to its leaders. This respect is evaluated and sustained by courtesies ranging from special provisions during conventions and conferences to titles which maintain the working relationship with the members. However this respect is demonstrated, Christians would do well to remember that respect for each other is a clear biblical command (Eph 5:21). However, very few pastors are known by their first names or become accessible socially to their members. Leaders and members don't always enjoy the same degree of rapport outside the worship event, in society. In many situations the failure to use an acknowledged title may be seen as a direct affront to personal authority and may be treated accordingly. Where the use of titles is important for our churches, ministers' main concern should not be with *personal* recognition alone. The more important issue is to ensure that people do not depart from a biblical understanding of respect for leadership.

Currently the black church is faced with a challenge of cultural transition. Parents and leading ministers often equate these basic courtesies with proper respect and good manners. However, young Christians brought up in the questionable values of a society in which lecturers, managers, royalty and prime ministers are known by their Christian names find it hard to equate respect with titles alone. Not surprisingly, many young Christians struggle to relate the truth of biblical authority to their world. And while titles are biblical, our use of them in and outside church buildings does not necessarily convey genuine respect any more than formality does in the House of Commons!

The man or woman in the pulpit must recognise that authority cannot be *demanded*: it must be *commanded* by the quality and integrity of one's ministry. Church members must recognise that respect for leadership is a biblical injunction and vital in a worshipping community. A pastor must never hide behind titles; members must never undervalue the pastor because they come to know him or her as a person. What is at stake, then, is the issue of human egos and a willingness to sacrifice personal preferences and prejudices for biblical relationships within the *worship-encounter* between those who lead and those who are led. If the pastor understands this he or she will not assess the use of titles in merely personal terms. Biblical principles and responses should be the guiding factors. Indeed, very few Christians—black or white—link titles with respect; consider names like Billy Graham, Morris Cerrullo, Paul Yonggi Cho and Oral Roberts. Surely it is conceivable that we may come to know our leaders without losing respect? In biblical perspective titles do not *give* respect; they *reflect* it. A proper response to authority is not determined by Afro-Caribbeans or by Europeans; rather, it is an essential part of the worship culture of those who belong to the kingdom.

The preacher's culture, and true worship

This issue of ministerial authority is vital to any understanding of the pulpit response to worship. A pastor plays a key role in setting the tone of worship for the local church. It is an awesome responsibility little understood by many occupants of the pulpit. From the pulpit, values pour into the congregation colouring the

stream of praise as it flows into the life of the fellowship. That stream may be polluted by false doctrines
or shallow and meaningless expressions. It may be
influenced by biblical truths and rich sounds of adoration. From the pulpit we may utter notes of praise that
embrace the cultural range of those present—or we may
alienate large numbers of young Christians or visitors
with ideas and language that distract the mind and
frustrate worship.

Since the pastor is the product of his or her up-
bringing, the worship of God is inevitably mediated
through the preacher's own cultural understanding of
worship. The responsible minister must therefore at
least *attempt* to separate culture from true worship. The
task undertaken by the early church is easily under-
estimated after two thousand years of church history
(Acts 15). It was a decision to 'deculturalise' or 'multi-
culturalise' the gospel. On the day of Pentecost the
multi-cultural listeners (albeit Jews and Israelites) heard
the praise of God in their own native languages. In fact
communicating the essentials of the Christian faith was
an enormous task which involved cultural, theological
and liturgical trauma for the early apostles. Jews were
challenged to appreciate that Gentiles could be true
worshippers. True worship, then, is worship that transcends the temporary trappings of cultural or denominational obligations and brings the human spirit to rest in
the presence of a God whose essential nature is love and
holiness. Denominations dilate and cultures change, but
God will always have true worship.

So although the preacher will be most at home with
what is culturally familiar, he or she must never be blind
to the universal worship of 'the God of all flesh'. If the
world is truly my parish, then it must never be alienated

from my pulpit by my *indifference* to other cultures. The pulpit response to worship in this regard is (as we've already seen) clearly set out in the principles of the Sychar well conversation (Jn 4). The pulpit must lead in the *deculturalisation* of worship in such a way that the preacher's own culture is not destroyed. In the presence of God there is room for everyone. The young black British must find room for his own black-Anglo culture. Visitors who may not fully relate to the ethos of the black worship style should, ideally, be able to identify some faint reflection of themselves in our act of worship.

Too often, leaders pass on their own cultural worship norms as though they were biblical imperatives. A Caribbean-style leadership valid in the West Indies may not always be relevant to a multi-cultural urban setting. Of course this approach from the pulpit is never made with selfish intent; it comes from a genuine desire to do things as we know them and in the conviction that they have been greatly used by God in the past. But familiarity can so easily inspire a sense of security that does not motivate us to aspire to new things.

In recent years the cultural expression of Afro-Caribbean worship has been the object of academic studies and has become more familiar. Its exuberance, spontaneity and emphatically Pentecostal nature has not only provided a caricature for the media but has also contributed to the renewal of other evangelical groups in the United Kingdom. These positive elements must never be lost; they are inalienable from a worship culture which has been shaped by the combination of an African heritage and the Holiness Pentecostal movement.

Most churches are bound by denominational worship norms, and every church group struggles with the responsibility to maintain a coherent but distinct liturgy. This has been one of the chief preoccupations of the Church of England in recent years, for example, as it attempts to retain the spirit of the Prayer Book without the obscure language of its original authors. Afro-Caribbean churches, too, have an order of service, one which has been maintained by an oral tradition no less binding than the written guidelines of many formal liturgies. The pastor stands in the pulpit as a denominational representative. He or she must have a genuine commitment to the distinctives of that particular group. Only the leader with a strong personal conviction can wander outside the usual pattern of worship without a feeling of betrayal!

The pastor who wishes to lead people into true worship must blaze a precarious path between the necessary demands of his or her denomination and worship that brings the people into fresh and frequent experiences of praise without prejudice or pretence.

From pew to pulpit

Any discussion on the pulpit response to worship in the black church must include an understanding of the process of ordination. It is very unusual for a relatively unknown person to enter the pulpit. The pastor does not normally enter the local ministry after having 'migrated' from another denomination. Neither is he or she parachuted into the church from the clouds of academia. Any minister accepted within the local church has usually withstood the scrutiny of the denominational microscope and had his preaching vetted by the doctrinal scruples of fellow ministers and the general membership.

There is little surprise when someone emerges as a pastor. In the black church, ministry is usually born out of the womb of the local church. The congregation gives its corporate assent through opportunities for lay ministry in its various departments. Ministry is assessed during the testimony, exhortation or choir participation and nurtured in the prayer meeting and Sunday School until it emerges and is 'set forth' by the local church. Training is not necessarily set aside. Many churches have their own training programmes, but formal training is invariably the *fine-tuning* of the pastoral call rather than its *finality*.

To obtain the people's commendation, the pastor must normally have proved himself or herself to be faithful in doctrine and presence. They cannot afford to stray from the fundamentals of an evangelical faith. A non-worshipping candidate is unlikely to pass the test. The pulpit and the pew engage, therefore, in a dynamic dialogue. The black preaching style frequently demands and depends on a call-response interaction typified by the preacher's call, 'Praise God!' or 'Let's praise him!'.

W.A. Blair's preaching during his UK visit from Jamaica in 1990 became firmly associated with the call, 'Hello! Are you there?' It is true that this call-response is sometimes the result of nervousness or uncertainty, but in its purest moments the calling is something far deeper. It is not a call for mere verbal response; instead, the preacher challenges the congregation to affirm the truth of the spoken word as it informs and affects worship.

'Dialogical preaching', as Martin Simmonds[1] describes it, was also depicted by an African preacher as a *dance* sustained by a significant level of verbal worship exchange between the pulpit and the pew. It involves the participation of ordinary members charged with the responsibility of 'helping the preacher'. A responsive church will read the preacher's text aloud, offer an appropriate concluding sentence or Bible verse. An elderly woman praying on Easter Sunday once gave God thanks for 'this Good Friday's Sunday'. That became the preacher's theme for the day!

This point of contact between the preacher and the people is often electrified by a mutual awareness of key Bible texts. Certain key texts celebrating concepts of liberation, victory, healing or the return of Christ ignite worship in the people. By the same token, the preacher is never at his best when detached from the people, and even the physical position of the pulpit is important. Where the podium may be placed in an inaccessible position in the building, the preacher will often alter his relationship by adopting a roving ministry moving among the people during the sermon.

This corporate preaching ethos is important. Preaching or the word of exhortation is not the exclusive privilege of the clergy. Pulpit participation becomes the expression of the body in worship. The main responsibility is always with the pastor, bishop or elder, but pulpit participation is often a joint responsibility. In some churches *anyone* may be called upon to preach or testify at a moment's notice!

Undoubtedly, this practice has its own hazards: a congregation may be subjected to untutored thoughts or poor doctrinal teaching. However, if dialogical preaching is pursued with care, it is a powerful process that affirms the whole body in worship. Defective presentations can be compensated for by the affirmation of the value of each person in the local church. Inadequacy is not the same as heresy. God is never compatible with false doctrines, but he is always present in our inadequacies. The most acceptable worship is often that which comes out of a single-minded commitment, which gives God an opportunity to be glorified in our imperfections. It is not always the clinically precise offering that warms the heart of God. We do not have to be perfect in order that God may accept us; we only have to be perfectly available. Also, we do not have to be perfect to be saved, but we do have to be saved to be perfect!

The language of worship

Carol Tomlin's study *Black Preaching Styles*[2] is a useful contribution to the growing collection of accounts of the black church in Britain. Although she gives her attention specifically to patterns of Jamaican preaching in Britain, the points which emerge are applicable to the entire black church culture.

The importance of the oral tradition and the impact of Africanisms in the oral tradition of Afro-Caribbean preaching mean that spontaneity and improvisation are crucial to black preachers, but this dependency on oral tradition has its problems. Even the most gifted speakers have bad moments when the stream of inspiration runs slowly. A rambling preacher without content or context is no more helpful to a congregation than the desperate screams of a drowning man, and the two things are not entirely dissimilar!

In many instances the preacher's reliance on spontaneity is nothing more than a camouflage for laziness or the reluctance to prepare a sermon well. A preacher coming to the pulpit with minimum preparation is easily swept along by the enthusiasm of a responsive congregation or intimidated by the silence of a more thoughtful non-response, but the energy of the people's participation may in fact produce little more from the preacher than repetitions of the things they want to hear. That kind of preaching fails to be prophetic and is unlikely to lead to any new areas of development. A church is not *necessarily* worshipping because it responds to pet phrases and familiar stories calculated to incite response so that the speaker may feel better about himself.

Nevertheless, oral tradition coupled with personal devotion and application is a powerful and authentic preaching style clearly present in the New Testament. It is conducive to the immediacy of the hour and adapts itself to our changing needs during the course of worship. It is not compromised by momentary diversions from the main theme of the sermon and can accommodate instant revelation and inspired knowledge. It allows the preacher to be many things to many people and still remain true to the proclamation of a central theme.

Such an approach facilitates the ebb and flow of the human spirit as the preacher becomes actively involved in the declaration of the good news. Its affinity with the New Testament maintains the preaching culture of the apostles, who used this same means to proclaim the gospel. The apostles 'preached the word' without clinical homiletical tools, and ordinary members 'gossiped the gospel' throughout Asia. Their knowledge of the written Law and their cultural appreciation for the spoken word was that effective combination which invariably led to the worship response of the hearers. Peter's first sermon drew over two thousand penitent worshippers (Acts 2). His opening statements at Cornelius' house resulted in the outpouring of the Holy Spirit across the cultural boundaries (Acts 10:44–46).

There is in these examples a definite relationship between the spontaneous declaration of the word and a
worshipping response.

Pentecostal preaching in general and black preaching
in particular expects a worship response. Invariably, the
language of the preacher shows this because the sermon
tends to be punctuated with shouts of 'Hallelujah', 'Amen'
or 'Praise the Lord!' Even where this becomes a habit
developed as a sedative for nervous tension, it shows the
worship vocabulary of the black preaching style.

Content and the pulpit

Preaching in the black church is demanding, not necessarily in terms of its exegetical precision or homiletical
orthodoxy but in terms of the presence of Christ in the
spoken word. Black preaching has indeed often been
accused of lacking theological content. It must be
admitted that examples of shallow biblical exposition
abound; and, given the humble background of most
black ministers who began in the 1950s and 1960s, this
may be expected. There is an evident lack of serious
expository teaching, and many ministers are paying the
price of their own neglect as young people leave black
churches in search of what is often described as 'solid
teaching'.

This is a definite challenge for church leaders,
and it is unhelpful to assume that young Christians
always leave because of ingratitude or in pursuit
of a church with lower moral standards. Often, it is a
cry for a ministry which relates to their particular
situations and which offers them *relevant* content. A
dismissive attitude from the pulpit makes no room
for self-examination or an assessment of the pulpit
response to the needs of the local congregation.

The black preaching style is conducive to dialogue between the pulpit and the pew and lends itself to the type of content that may be said to typify the majority of black preachers. On the whole, black preachers in the United States, Caribbean and the UK are extemporaneous preachers who follow an intuitive flow of biblical ideas and text around a particular theme. For complex reasons there is very little systematic expository preaching in a black church. In the first instance, an oral culture is less likely to be attracted to a cerebral and contemplative sermon which relies on a formal theological background. Very simply, few ministers were supplied with the tools of theological reflection in their formative years. An oral culture sits more comfortably, therefore, with a preaching method that draws from the wealth of personal experience and intuitive knowledge rather than from received information. Black preaching tends to be more celebratory than cerebral. This does not mean, however, that the authority of Scripture is swept aside or replaced by human intuition: it means that the authenticity of Scripture has been cross-referenced by personal experience and preached in the light of that reality.

As Arlington Trotman so clearly described in Chapter 1, black church preaching has its genesis in a development of Holiness-Pentecostal history that shied away from a nineteenth-century church stunned by the effects of humanistic, secular rationalism. This was the environment in which many clergymen with academic distinctions failed to transmit the presence of God in the words they spoke from the pulpit. Pentecostal-Holiness preaching of the day was a direct rejection of secular Christianity and of dependence on precise words above the experienced Word. In its early stages, Pentecostal preachers—both black and white—positively resisted the use of notes in the pulpit! Undoubtedly such a preaching style was easily assimilated into the oral culture of black preachers.

Although it is true to say that extemporaneous delivery typifies black preachers, it is equally important to recognise that there has been a significant counter trend in the direction of the more 'considered sermon' over the last ten years. This has been stimulated by the proliferation of small Bible schools in the black church community, the wider exposure of the clergy, and an increasingly better informed laity. Many black preachers have committed themselves—often at great personal and family costs—to the systematic and formal study of the Scriptures to improve their range of preaching content. No doubt there will always be individuals who insist, 'Open your mouth and the Lord will fill it!' Given the present developments in our society and churches, however, such a ministry is guaranteed a relatively short life-span.

Having outlined the urgent need for an up-grading of theological content in much of the preaching, we must also acknowledge the vitality of the existing theology— always an important part of the preaching. This is not the classical theology of the historic churches; it is *vital theology* conveyed in the hymns that have been an integral part of the preaching. What Charles Wesley did for teaching in Methodism, Sankey and Moody have done for the black church. Hymns are woven into the fabric of the preachers' material, reinforcing biblical truth and forming a vital theological lifeline to the believer, whose knowledge of them has been treasured in the tradition of the spoken word. The spiritual life of many people with low reading ability has been sustained by a diet of key Bible texts and popular hymns that together act as a critical point of contact between the pulpit and the pew, informing and reinforcing faith and worship.

Similarly, the storytelling content of the sermon, properly understood, is essentially a method of verbal indoctrination used so effectively by Christ and the early church leaders. Storytelling is not myth; it stimulates faith in the historic reliability of the Bible which demands a simplicity of faith. Worship becomes the natural response of a person who recognises his or her circumstances in the ordinary outline of the extraordinary story of the Cross. The repetition of a well-known story is not unbiblical. Even when it may not be *informative*, this type of preaching may be *affirmative* as it consolidates faith and enhances worship.

The priority of preaching

A standard ice-breaking joke made by many visiting preachers relates to the fact that black preachers tend to preach longer than twenty minutes! The average preaching time is between forty and sixty minutes. Without the inspirational flow, that hour in the pulpit can be a long time for the listener. The primacy of preaching is clearly shown by the time allotted to it. Preaching stands at the pinnacle of worship and dominates a third of the time. Effectively other activities act as preparatory steps to the altar of the declared word.

The black church shares this characteristic with other evangelical groups, but the issue is of particular significance in the context of the black church. Everything builds up to the sermon and acts as the platform on which the sermon is built. People are expected to 'continue in the attitude of worship' in receiving the preacher. In turn the preacher may stimulate continued worship with a song or prayer before, during or after the sermon.

The preacher as worshipper

The role of chief worshipper is inseparable from that of the preacher. The preacher is disqualified if he or she presents merely a theological discourse in the pulpit. Worship must be the mode of communication by which the gospel is transmitted. The preacher-pastor must explore and express the latent worship of the people, for the pulpit becomes the representative of the worship service and the point of integration for the people's adoration of Christ. In that moment, the minister carries the assent of the people as the chief worshipper. As Carol Tomlin expresses it: 'The Black preaching style is an integral part of the whole black worship experience and this has to be taken into account when unfolding the underlying meaning of this preaching.'[3]

Good preaching, then, is not determined by how clearly a reasoned argument has been presented for debate, but to what extent the truth of that argument has been enjoined and enjoyed by the preacher and how much his worship becomes infectious to the listener. The black church makes a clear distinction between a well presented talk on the resurrected Christ and a worshipping experience of the living Word.

Ethics and worship

An exploration of the ethical imperatives of the gospel is worthwhile here. As we have seen, worship is an inclusive term involving our total lifestyle before God, in and out of the church building. It is a life that ascribes *worth* to God, and such a lifestyle can never bypass the moral demands of Scripture.

For many reasons that we cannot deal with in one short chapter, the black church has emphasised the Holiness code as an integral part of Christian commitment that affects our social, sexual and church conduct. Strident sermons against sin in its varied expressions are common. Although there is a need for clearer definitions of sin and holiness based more specifically on biblical principles rather than on traditional prejudices, there is no doubting the commitment to a Christian lifestyle which affects moral conduct. This emphasis on Christian ethics thus induces an understanding of worship which affects our ethical conduct. In the aftermath of slavery, the black church has been consistent in preaching a message that attempts to salvage self-respect from the debris of a shattered people. This message is still valid in the moral uncertainties of a secular society. It is the hallmark of the Holiness tradition, which is inseparable from morality, and is the bedrock of the black church ethos.

Even when some theological distinctives are hard to identify and articulate, black Christians are clear about the pulpit expectations on issues of moral conduct. A young woman recently recalled a story she'd heard fifteen years earlier as a girl of eight: her pastor had told of a little girl in the Caribbean who was always embarrassed by her untidy desk when the school inspector visited unexpectedly. The girl concluded that the only safe option was to keep her desk tidy at all times. 'From that early age,' said the young woman, 'the story came through to me: I must keep my life clean before God all the time, because I never know when Christ is coming.'

This lifestyle is the essence of worshipful living. The

demand for constant cleansing by Christ is the emblem
of holiness and authentic worship. The preacher stands
as the proclaimer of a Monday-to-Saturday worship
lifestyle, which leads the worshipper to 'true worship'
in the sanctuary on Sunday morning.

Practical applications for the pulpit

As the chief worshipper, the preacher has an awesome
task. He or she must develop a spiritual maturity able
to discern between the demands of our denominational
background and the conditioning of cultural preferences. This life-time task depends on the wisdom of God
but may also be reinforced by some practical steps on
our part.

There is an *obligation* to take sufficient time in which
to understand the 'cultural language' of non-Caribbeans
and black British youth. The children in our homes may
be a very good starting point! It could be so refreshing
to hear more preachers asking a child or young adult,
'What do you mean?' It would also be liberating to hear
them say, 'I don't understand.' It is a sad truth that
people who talk a lot seldom listen, and most preachers
have a lot to say.

Preachers also need to develop a community con-
sciousness. Even where they may not have the time
or skill to be engrossed in community issues, black
preachers must understand those issues in order to
speak with relevance and power. Jesus was a street-man
who spoke the language of the street with a Galilean
accent. A wider vision of the community and the world
rescues preaching from the claustrophobic issues within
the church walls and releases the gospel to the ends of
the earth. A man or woman from the streets will

recognise the gospel when the language of the street is spoken from the pulpit. In effect, that was the point of contact with the outsiders on the day of Pentecost as each person heard the disciples 'declaring the wonders of God in our own tongues!' (Acts 2:11).

Sensitive and informed ministry becomes aware that the black church is a missionary concern in the urban harvest. It would be sad if black Christians who in the past rightly reacted to the colonisation of our minds and cultures by Western missionaries now pursued a path of cultural exclusiveness that put newcomers into a Caribbean cultural straightjacket in order for their worship to become acceptable. Inevitably a dominant culture will and should make its mark upon the worship culture of a local church; however, the minister's task is not to submit all cultures to the dictates of the majority culture, but to ensure the skilful and prayerful weaving of all sections. Thus the varying shades of cultural diversity are mixed into the tapestry of worship in a way which most members find conducive to worship.

In an ideal situation, an Asian member of a black church should not be required to become a non-Asian for five hours each Sunday any more than a Caribbean should cease to be so in an Anglican church. If white Christians in a black church insist on clapping *on* the beat during worship, perhaps they should be allowed to—even if it upsets the drummer's sensibilities!

God has called us to work and worship in the urban context. He also calls us to lead others 'to glorify our Father in heaven'. Worship is the essence of an adoration, which is concerned primarily neither with customs nor cultures but with truth and sincerity. This was the basic message of Jesus' conversation with the Samaritan

Woman at Jacob's Well, a discourse that found greater expression in the great Jerusalem Council of Acts 15. 'It seemed good to the Holy Spirit and to us,' said the Jewish worshippers, 'not to burden you with anything beyond the following. . . . abstain from food sacrificed to idols, from blood, from meat of strangled animals and from sexual immorality' (Acts 15:28–29). The message was clear: Gentiles could be Gentiles and yet be true worshippers.

Dynamic worship cannot be static; it moves and breathes, harmonising the reality of the people's experiences with the reality of God. As their experience changes, so their expressions of gratitude will change. It is unlikely that Jacob's worship was identical to Noah's. Solomon's temple worship was far more involved than that of his forefather, Jacob. In each case, they drew from the acquired wealth of Israel's worship history and made the worship of Yahweh their own within the context of the things they now knew about worship. The Jewish worshippers in the Upper Room became distinctive from the people in the synagogues of Nazareth or the priests in the Temple at Jerusalem. The worship leader called Simon Peter had experienced a revolutionary concept of worship by the time he visited the Italian Christians in Cornelius' house (Acts 10).

The pulpit stands as the focal point between the mere preservation of a cultural status quo and vital, biblical worship. The preacher is never called to abandon the hallmarks of the majority culture in the interest of some naive notion of a non-cultural Christianity. Black pastors bowed down with a sense of shame regarding their own worship norms suffer from an inadequate awareness of the richness of their cultural history and the penalties of incipient racism. It would be a serious travesty if black worship made unnatural and forced attempts to be what it is not. Equally, it would be absurd for black leaders to insist on holding to the forms and liturgies of the past three decades at the expense of younger members who do not necessarily share the same liturgical culture. In the pulpit the black minister-worship-leader is charged with a solemn task. He or she must preserve the value and integrity of the people, affirming them in their identity, but also leading them from Jacob's Well to the Upper Room and beyond.

Notes

1. Martin Simmonds, *A Portrayal of Identity. A study of the Life of Worship of the First United Church of Jesus Christ (Apostolic) UK* (Unpublished M Phil dissertation: University of Birmingham, May 1988).
2. Carol Tomlin, *Black Preaching Style* (Unpublished M Phil dissertation: University of Birmingham, Oct 1988).
3. Ibid, p 131.

4

The Pentecostal Distinctives

Joel Edwards

Acts 2 gives a clear illustration of the experience of worship that accompanied the birth of the Christian church. It incorporated tongues (*glossolalia*), the dynamic interaction of extemporaneous preaching and crowd response, spontaneous worship, and the element of the unfamiliar. It was enough to make anyone believe that those involved were drunk—even though it was the wrong time of the day! Pentecostal worship does not need all of these elements to make it truly Pentecostal, but it is likely to include some of them if it is.

In this chapter we will attempt a brief review of some of the distinctive features of black Pentecostal worship. These more obvious characteristics may be regarded as the hallmarks of black Pentecostalism, but in many instances they are also typical of the broad spectrum of 'classical' or 'historic' Pentecostal churches. The purpose here is to provide a reflection on rather than a defence of the practices which black Pentecostals hold dear.

The liturgy of Pentecost

The word 'liturgy' describes the regular pattern of church worship or Eucharist. Each tradition has its own liturgy shaped by theological distinctives and cultural norms. Sometimes the two are woven together so tightly that they become inseparable. The Anglican Prayer Book (ASB), for instance, carries culture as well as theology.

Pentecostalism, including black Pentecostalism, has its own well formulated liturgy. To the uninitiated, black church worship may appear to be a random collection of spontaneous and apparently unrelated events. Choruses and hymns may not follow any particular theme. The preacher is likely to announce a text from which he wanders for significant periods of time. The participation of the congregation could set off a 'liturgical mood-swing' in unpredictable directions, or the service could close without a formal sermon as originally intended. However, the regular visitor has another story to tell. Short of divine intervention, the order of a church service can in fact be very predictable. Black church worship has an oral liturgy which may be described as *organised spontaneity*. In most cases it follows a typical pattern:

- *Devotional service*—including a hymn, prayer and Bible reading. In some churches the worship leader may precede this with a hymn or song before he or she 'hands over' to the devotional leader.
- *Further singing and testimonies* often take place during the evening service, which is longer than the morning worship.
- *Special prayer*—for sick or those needing ministry.
- *Offering*—which may be accompanied with a choir song or congregational singing.
- *Special singing*—from the choir, soloist or group. Invariably some congregational singing will take place immediately before the preacher. It is unusual for the preacher to come before the ground has been 'ploughed' with singing to prepare the hearts to 'receive the preacher'.
- *The sermon*—Once presented, the preacher is likely to

choose his or her own song. In some cases the sermon may be culled from an individual who was not prepared to preach before arriving at the service. A sermon may last from forty to sixty minutes.

- *The altar call*—both Christians and non-Christians will be given an opportunity to make an appropriate response to the preached word.

This pattern is an unwritten order of events immediately recognisable to a regular attender. It is a curious combination of immovable liturgical habits and a flexibility which allows scope for reshaping where necessary. In many churches, for example, it would be unacceptable to conclude the Bible reading without adding: 'Glory be to the Father and to the Son and to the Holy Ghost. As it was in the beginning it now and ever shall be. World without end. Amen.'

Words of this nature are of course part of a liturgical construction familiar to Anglicans. If this more formal response is omitted, the readings may be punctuated with 'May the Lord add his blessings to the reading of his word', or 'We say, "Amen!"' may be substituted. Similarly, it is unusual to have the offering without prayer either immediately before or after it has been received. In black church worship, few services are concluded without a formal benediction. Evidently, black Pentecostalism, like any other tradition, is committed to a liturgical formula so as to maintain coherence and a framework that everyone involved may use as a point of reference.

The scope for reshaping comes from the church's openness to the needs of the people and the inspirational flow of the service. It is further facilitated by a degree of flexibility in attitudes to time-keeping. People are usually prepared to over-run a church service if what is happening is thought profitable. Much of this development is the combined interaction between the worship leader, the preacher and the congregation. As we noted in Chapter 3, the responsive dialogue between the worship leader and the people is a vital component in the worship. Black Pentecostalism can never be satisfied with passive non-response; it demands encounter, for worship is an encounter with God in harmony with others. A non-responsive audience is likely to evoke from the pulpit 'I can't feel you!' or 'Let's praise him.' It is the equivalent to the 'Can I have a witness?' in the black churches of America. This *witness* is the combined agreement to the vitality of a liturgy which truly believes that the letter may kill but 'the Spirit giveth life' (2 Cor 3:6).

Music and worship

As in most worship settings, music plays a central role. In many black churches it dominates worship, creating the sense of movement and spontaneity. Songs punctuate the various segments of worship and creatively camouflage any restless moments in the order of events.

As stated elsewhere, in the traditional black church, hymns still underpin biblical teaching and make doctrine accessible to the worshipper. Preachers quote songs or choruses as readily as Bible texts. Songs set the scene for the sermon and act as a concluding feature of the preacher's address. In some cases, a relevant hymn or chorus enhances a focal point *during* a sermon. This was powerfully illustrated by the preacher, Lennox Powell, when during a sermon on the Crucifixion he spontaneously led the congregation in a well-known song based on Isaiah's prophetic statement:

> He was wounded for our transgression
> He was bruised for our iniquity
> Surely, he hath borne our sorrow
> And by his stripes we are healed.[1]

In the black church the *song* is the worship property of all members, who may use it to express their deepest joys or sorrows. Those least comfortable with words will often 'borrow the words of the song' to express their experience. Indeed, Iain MacRobert contends that in the black church the song is one of the most unifying and peculiar features of the church's life. This he regards as one of the distinguishing marks of black worship, one which has survived its cross-Atlantic passage from Africa via America and the Caribbean. This dependence on song is one of the unique characteristics of black Christianity, and gives it a universal coherence. (MacRobert is comfortable about using the term 'Black Church' as this, he feels, properly identifies the churches that share this common liturgical feature.)[2] The significance of negro spirituals and songs in the black American experience has also been usefully documented by many writers including James Cone in his *God of the Oppressed* and *Spirituals and the Blues*.

Even the more articulate rely on songs as an acceptable mode of communicating their true feelings. The song provides a legitimate alternative for the spoken testimony. As a result, it is not unusual to hear someone say, 'For my testimony, I would like to sing. . . .' This is not an abdication of personal testimony or necessarily an unwillingness to speak. It is simply a recognition that the song has already fully represented one's own thoughts in an art form conducive to worship. It is both real and biblical.

In recent years much has been written about the slavery heritage and the use of song. Undoubtedly, black Pentecostalism has inherited much of the culture conveyed through the negro spirituals. This influence has certainly stamped a quality of 'other-worldness' to the liturgy of the black church. 'Separatedness' is also deeply imbedded in the songs, influenced by a curious combination of the revivalism of the Southern States Holiness movement of the nineteenth century and the survivalism of the American negro in slavery. It is important to recognise that this emphasis is not wholly negative. As we will discuss later, the longing for a better world that still pours from popular songs was the source of a valuable hymnology of anticipation. The slaves' hope was as real as their suffering, and in a sense the song became a means of salvation.

The message of hope has been aided by the repetitive style of the music, which lends itself to a powerful form of oral indoctrination. Historically black churches have been associated with the poor. Consequently, it has been a main education centre for thousands of black people, their education coming from the Bible and the spoken word. Because repetition is both biblical and practical, it reinforces truth and seals abstract concepts in the mind. Black pentecostal worship has drawn deeply from this historic well to water the tired spirits of its adherents, whose natural method of learning was the spoken, repetitive word.

Currently a powerful transition is taking place in Pentecostal worship. This change is coming about largely through the music of the younger Christians. The traditional hymns of Sankey and Moody and the

Redemption Hymnal are quietly giving way to the American choir sound. Even the more recent Country Western style of the Chuck Wagon Gang[3] and popular denominational hymnals loved by many senior adults is gently being set aside for the more contemporary sounds of black American songs or the worship chorus culture of British Christian songwriters like Graham Kendrick.

The wealth of creative talent which has learned and faithfully reproduced black American gospel music is having the greatest single impact on the worship of black churches today. Relatively few churches are without a gospel or youth choir; a Sunday morning comparison between the youth choir and the senior adult choir tells its own story. Moreover, there are very few churches in which young adults are being fed from the youth choir into the senior adult choir. The average age of a senior choir is likely to be over forty-five, with little hope of survival beyond the next ten years. This means that black Pentecostalism in Britain will lose a part of its identity that was very prominent in the 1960s and 1970s. The quartet and hymnal culture is seriously under threat of extinction in some sectors of the church.

Evidently, some adults would argue that this older style is the authentic 'sound of Zion' and therefore the true representation of black Pentecostal worship. However, as mentioned earlier, many of these hymns were borrowed from a combination of old negro spirituals, Southern States writers of early Pentecostalism, and from the strong influences of mainstream churches. In each case these selections were further transformed by the oral traditions and culture of Caribbean Christians, which gave them a rhythm and movement never intended by the original songwriters! The biblical truths of these great hymns were owned but their mood was subject to cultural surgery when the songs reached the Caribbean.

The truly authentic Caribbean song is to be found much more in the numerous choruses known throughout the black church that have no identifiable author. They convey a distinct cultural and worship environment which is unmistakably Caribbean—they are even sometimes exclusive to particular pockets of the Caribbean:

> Better get right with God.
> Come and do it now,
> Under the Cross of Jesus—
> Lay your burdens down.
> Better get right with God.
> Come and do it now.
> Get right, get right—
> Better get right with God.

Such a song incorporates a bold simplicity and urgency conveyed by the repetitive and uncompromising directness; it is the confrontation of the Cross. The song lives because it harmonises simple words with a compulsive melody. Only a spiritually indifferent person hears this chorus, understands it, and still rejects the Cross.

This kind of worship is in danger of extinction. The electronic age of musical sophistication has little interest in simplicity. Black church music is moving very fast; Andre Crouch and the Disciples are 'old', and the gospel circuit has long since pushed him aside to make room for the popular mass choirs or the more contemporary sounds of the Winans, BeBe and CeCe and Commissioned. The song is becoming the music, not necessarily the message; talent rather than testimony has become the new measurement by which the song is judged. In itself the performance of musical ability presents no problem, but black churches must give urgent attention to this issue lest the contribution of its most gifted musicians and writers fails to make a lasting impact on worship and the gap between the Saturday night gospel concert and Sunday morning worship becomes an uncrossable chasm.

Another important transition is taking place in black Pentecostalism. As many young adults become assimilated into the mainstream of academic and professional life, their liturgical requirements are changing. Many churches are therefore facing the challenges for a more cerebral song—that is, a worship setting with identifiable elements of order and thought in the midst of the spontaneity. Young adults in Britain are the product of Western rationalism. They are conditioned by study and work to value ideas presented rationally. This does not mean a denial of the intuitive or miraculous, but there is undoubtedly a search for worship nearer to their own (changing) identity. The culture of new worship choruses from charismatic Christians has become a recent development in black Pentecostalism. Old songbooks compete with the chorus book and overhead projector! The meaning may be the same, but the song is changing.

The body in worship

Black Pentecostalism has never been preoccupied with a theological explanation of the 'priesthood of all believers' or with the concept of body ministry. However, it has to some extent articulated these biblical principles in its worship. Many churches are typified by strong leadership—sometimes approaching autocracy. At the same time this has been counteracted by extensive lay participation in the worship, which informs and runs through the texture of black Pentecostalism. The one-man show is virtually unknown because the range of activities has always included a broad sweep of individual, group and congregational contributions, all of which rescue the worship from vocal monotony.

There is, for example, the frequent participation of the ordinary member during the testimony service. Depending on the flow of testimonies, this part of the worship can dominate the event and even eclipse the formal preaching. Testimonies are not rehearsed presentations. A service will be 'left open' for voluntary contributions from members or Christian visitors who may wish to participate. 'In my church,' said one English visitor in a black church, 'we would need to have a week's notice to do this sort of thing. But anyway, I'll do my best!' Usually testimony has little to do with status or experience. It is a first-stand, first-talk situation where even the youngest member of the congregation will be affirmed in his or her own witness of the Resurrection story.

The role of women

The place of women is worth a mention in this context. Of course a chapter on Pentecostal distinctives of worship cannot afford the luxury of a detailed explanation of a Pentecostal theology of gender; but the ambiguity of the place of women in Pentecostalism *is* important. Pentecostalism has a rather strained relationship which reveals the prominence of women. Mary Campbell, a member of Edward Irving's Presbyterian church, was the first person in England to speak in tongues during the 1830s.[4] On 1st January 1901 Agnes Osman, an eighteen-year-old American woman received the baptism of the Holy Spirit and provided the first twentieth-century record of speaking in tongues, which gave credence to Parham's teachings of 'initial evidence' (speaking in tongues came to be regarded as the first evidence of baptism in the Holy Spirit). That happening in the Bethel Bible School at Topeka, Kansas, set a small flame to the spiritual inferno which raged in Azusa Street (in Los Angeles) between 1906 and 1909 under the black man, William J. Seymour. From then onwards, Pentecostalism has been aided by the committed tenacity and invaluable ministries of women like Aimee McPherson, Phoebe Palmer, Mrs Cantel and Mrs Woodworth Etter, whom Donald Gee described as 'the first personality to become prominent in the line of great evangelistic and divine healing revivals in the States . . .'.[5] Meanwhile the Church of God began as the Christian Union; eight people responded to R.G. Spurling's appeal on the 19th August 1886 to begin a new movement, of whom five were women.[6]

As Ira Brooks has stated: 'The true value of women in black-led Pentecostalism has never been faced squarely.'[7] Similarly, Io Smith, the black woman pastor, has given her own account of prejudices experienced from colleagues from within black Pentecostalism.[8] Evidence now exists to show that the combination of societal attitudes to women, the reexamination of biblical principles of interpretation and the sheer weight of numbers are all causing Pentecostals to review the role of women in the liturgical provisions of the church. In the Church of God, for example, significant strides were made to permit all female pastors full ministerial rights, although the full question of ordination is another debate still to be fully pursued.[9]

In black churches, women have on one level enjoyed a good deal of participation, both through the almost mandatory ladies' departments, and through their prominence in song-leading and activities during those Sundays designated 'ladies' Sunday'. In most churches the idea of a woman pastor has been well established for many years. Paradoxically, women have seldom exercised the rites of the priestly office and so have been barred from conducting the Lord's Supper, dedicating babies or baptising converts. Yet, ironically, no biblical sanctions have been invoked on women teachers, preachers or pastors despite the evidence of Paul's statement (1 Tim 2:12). On another level women are invariably not permitted to assume ultimate responsibility for any organisational structures or to participate in the strictly sacramental duties of the church's worship life.

This ambiguity highlights a thin line of confusion between irrational prejudices, biblical objections and the way in which the two things may easily become confused. It also reveals a very important worship distinctive of Pentecostalism: the Pentecostal church is not sacramental (in the sense of focusing primarily on the Eucharist) and, therefore, the concept of leadership is not necessarily centred on the idea of a mediating priesthood. In the sacramental liturgy of many historic churches leadership becomes synonymous with ordination and Eucharist. In Pentecostalism the two are not necessarily the same. The leader is not inevitably the priest-figure because all become mediators in their own right. In theory, at least, *anyone* can 'bless' another person. However, in the execution of the 'high office' of the ordinances, the issue of gender does become very significant. It is at this point that terminal irony sets in, for the only texts marshalled in opposition to a woman at a Communion table will be those biblical texts which are overlooked in relation to a woman's role as a teacher, preacher or pastor! To put it another way, Pentecostalism turns a blind eye to Paul's statements about women in the church in areas of teaching, preaching, praying, prophesying or pastoring, but it will activate those same texts in the areas of the Lord's Supper, baptism, marriages or even the dedication of infants.

This contradiction within the worshipping body points to a very important liturgical issue. Women, who form the majority of the worship setting, seldom participate in the formal areas of their church's liturgical life. The point here is neither in defence or justification but because it is important. If women's creative spiritual energies are precluded from the centre stage of the most sacred worship duties, they must presumably find powerful expression in other areas of the worship setting.

Because the minister does not bear sole responsibility for the preaching ministry in the local church, the 'word of exhortation' by which others may deliver 'sermonettes' is a popular feature. Whole Sundays are invariably given over to a particular department of the local church, so others are given access to the pulpit. In so doing, ministries which would otherwise pass unnoticed are given opportunities to come to light.

In the black church many contributions are either preceded or concluded with the request, 'Please pray for me in Jesus' Name.' Prayer has always been a communal exercise. The intercessor prays on behalf of others and 'takes us to the throne of grace'. In Pentecostalism the intercessor does not go to God alone. Audible responses during individual prayers signal to the intercessor that she is indeed surrounded by a great crowd of witnesses; that prayer is usually sanctioned by the strong 'Amen!'. Possibly more than any other section of the Christian family, black churches practise corporate congregational prayer. It is not unusual to hear the worship leader direct, 'Let's all talk to the Lord together.' Such an act of mass outpouring can be noisy and perplexing. It can also be a powerful reminder of the implied New Testament model of Acts, when the apostles' prayer was followed by a profound shaking of the Holy Spirit (Acts 4:29–31).

Pentecostalism and ordinances

An ordinance is a religious rite of a church community performed by an authorised minister. In this area, potent traditional influences have crossed denominational and liturgical frontiers to make a lasting impact on black churches. Some of these have already been noted.

Footwashing

Among the practices is that of 'washing the saints' feet'. Generally, black Pentecostals follow a literal interpretation of Christ's example of washing the disciples' feet (Jn 13:2–17) and see in it an obligation which transcends culture and time. There is little clear biblical teaching on the subject during the worship setting, but there can be no doubting the sincerity of the commitment to this supreme example of selfless servanthood. Usually, the congregation splits up into separate groups for males and females. Individuals wash one another's feet using a bowl with a towel to wipe the feet.

Theological objections to the practice rest on the assumption that the event recorded by John was merely an example of Jewish hospitality and hygiene. The suggestion is that such an act was necessary, particularly before a Jewish meal. In any event, it is deemed inadvisable to build an ordinance on this single reference with only the obscure text of 1 Timothy 5:10 to support it. While the latter point may be a textual stumbling-block there can be little doubt that a proper reading of John's account leaves us in no doubt that what Jesus did in washing his followers' feet *after* supper (Jn 13:4) was something far more significant than an act of hospitality or hygiene.

That footwashing is singularly unappealing may in fact cause the most opposition to it, rather than any meritorious biblical argument. However, it has a long history and was certainly included in the practices of Anabaptists in the sixteenth century. More recently a large, hitherto unknown, group of 900,000 Russian Pentecostals declared their surprise and delight in discovering another group who practised footwashing. For most black Pentecostals, then, it would appear that this distinctive ordinance has come via the Nonconformist church of the sixteenth century through the Holiness Movement of the late nineteenth century. Colin Whittaker's book, *Seven Pentecostal Pioneers*, cites the example of a Pentecostal missionary, William Burton, who used this ordinance with great effect as early as 1920 to reconcile opposing factions of his work in the Congo Evangelistic Mission.[10] Interestingly, increasing numbers of Christians are now reviewing their attitude to this ordinance.

Unfortunately, very little has been written on this ordinance—a fact that probably deserves its own detailed commentary. It is not enough to dismiss the passage in John 13 merely as a Jewish cultural quirk since the details of the text do not readily support such a superficial interpretation.[11] Those who stand opposed to the practice must themselves investigate the correctness of their own theological stance and cultural predispositions.

The Lord's Supper

Usually footwashing is immediately preceded by the Lord's Supper. There is a marked contrast between the solemnity of the Lord's Supper—which normally has a clear exposition—and the more light-hearted response to the footwashing. The Lord's Supper is usually reserved for those who have a clear personal Christian commitment. Pentecostals tend to put the emphasis on the experiential rather than the sacramental, and the former bears witness to the latter. The Lord's Table is therefore the celebration of Christ's presence, not only within the symbols of bread and wine, but also in the community of faith and worship. In the celebration of the Lord's Supper there is an expectation of the *felt presence* of the One who is remembered.

Baptism

Baptism is a genuinely communal experience. It is never a case of a minister 'doing' baptism, but an enactment of a dramatic theme where the pool becomes the focal point and the candidates become the symbolic representatives of all that Christ has done in each Christian believer. A baptismal service tends to generate an exciting environment, and in one sense the minister is merely acting as a conductor of the prevailing currents of expectancy.

Black Pentecostals do not practise infant baptism. It is always a conscious act by candidates who are thought old enough to make a conscious step of faith. A personal testimony of Christian commitment is given before baptism by full immersion. In most cases baptism is done using the Trinitarian wording of 'the Father, Son and Holy Spirit'. The exception to this rule is the 'Jesus Only' or Apostolic Churches who baptise only 'in the name of Jesus' and who may equate baptism with conversion. The community experience tends to be augmented by the attendance of relatives and friends of the candidate who are usually invited to witness the unique public demonstration of their Christian commitment. As a result, the service usually has a clear evangelistic thrust; it is expected that onlookers may be moved to make personal commitments of faith during the process of the worship.

Spirituality and worship

It goes without saying that Pentecostals have a particular regard for spiritual worship. That is why the text John 4:24 is so important to black Pentecostals, who fervently believe in worshipping 'in the spirit'. There is therefore no doubting the spiritual energy of our worship and preaching, but there is little room for complacency if that energy is to find its fullest and most mature expressions within our worship.

Pentecostal and Holiness churches are constantly engaged in a necessary search for a spirituality that retains the foundational beliefs of the nineteenth-century Holiness code without slipping out of touch with the twenty-first century. Hence Pentecostals have to discern the difference between symbols and reality. Those cultural emblems of holiness which emerged between 1920 and 1960 as the dividing lines between 'the world' and 'the church' subsequently (and sadly) became totally identified with biblical holiness. As the African proverb puts it: 'I pointed you to the moon and you only saw my finger!' True spirituality becomes measurable by external things, but a spirituality assessed *initially* or *primarily* by external observation cannot be regarded as biblical spirituality. And, inevitably, this emphasis on the external puts us at risk. A casual glance at a person's appearance cannot and must not be the determining measurement of a spiritual person, for it is likely to produce a very superficial spirituality.

All people are bound by cultural norms. Christians, therefore, have the burden of making responsible decisions between what is essential to spirituality and what is not; maturity seeks to determine the distinctions between a vital Christian culture and cultural expressions of Christianity. There will always be things that are cultural and changeable and other things that are fundamentally spiritual and eternal. The Holy Spirit is pleased to work within our cultural context, but he is not limited to it. God is concerned about what we look like, but he is far more concerned about who we are (see 1 Sam 16:7). We are indeed temples of the Spirit but the content is more important than the colour scheme! Spirituality therefore calls out for a discipline of mind and heart proportional to the intensity of our worship. The content of worship must be improved so that worship which is naturally powerful may be biblically understood. Few churches, for example, have any exposure to disciplined expository preaching or teaching on the great doctrines which form the cornerstones of the Christian faith. As Andrew Walker has suggested, there are very few Pentecostals—black or white—who understand their history or theology.[12]

It is sad that, in spite of the constant quest for spirituality, so few churches have any clear manifestations of spiritual gifts in their local congregations. Few ministers ever attempt a systematic teaching on the subject, and it is rare that church members are able to locate the passages in the Bible dealing with the subject.

Above all other gifts, the gift of tongues has emerged as the symbol of the Pentecostal lifestyle. This is largely because many traditional Pentecostals hold to the view that speaking in tongues is not only 'the initial evidence' of the baptism of the Holy Spirit, but also the observable evidence. Sometimes the people have gazed at the sign and missed the substance. The experience and practice of tongues has, therefore, become the line of demarcation between 'those who have it' and 'those who don't'. Though Pentecostalism has a right to insist on the importance of this experience, it also has a responsibility to avoid a two-tier system of Christianity separating those who have spoken in tongues and those who have not.

Challenges for black Pentecostalism

Black Pentecostalism has a clear challenge to help churches grow beyond the mark of the *initial evidence* of the Holy Spirit to the *substantial evidence* of Spirit-filled life. This may mean diverting energies away from the well-worn path of multiple programmes and internal activities towards the discipline of study, personal application and a corporate maturity in the use of spiritual gifts. There is a direct challenge not only to identify the gifts that are lying dormant within the congregation, but also actively to seek the development of other biblical gifts that seldom surface during the course of worship. The fact is that the label 'Pentecostal' in no way guarantees the fullness of true Pentecost in the life of a local congregation.

Teaching about a fruit-bearing lifestyle is also lacking. There is a paucity of direct information about the Christian character and fruit-bearing experience (Gal 5:22–23). Those vital traits of love, joy and peace are assumed rather than taught. In this respect Pentecostalism inclines towards the dramatic at the expense of disciplined behaviour. Superficial experiences often walk hand in hand with the dramatic. Pentecostal Christians need to hear again and again that God places greater value on fruit bearing than on dynamic manifestations; for when tongues cease, love will still endure (1 Cor 13:8). Only slowly are we learning that discipline in worship does not have to be dull, that power is not always loud, and that being orderly is not necessarily 'quenching the Spirit'.

Broadly speaking black Pentecostalism is faced with two major challenges. The first is the reassessment of its historic cultural influences and the second a re-evaluation of its understanding of spirituality. The spirituality of Pentecostalism emerged from the experiences of the Great Welsh Revival in 1904, the spiritual awakening in Europe and, more specifically, the Azusa Street outpouring in Los Angeles (1906–9). Institutional Pentecostalism, meanwhile, is as we've noted the off-spring of Southern American revival. It is against this backdrop that the second challenge must be faced. An

understanding of true spirituality may require abandoning some of 'the traditions of men' in order to find
the heart of God. God's 'cosmic generosity', as J.I.
Packer describes it, must therefore embrace all cultures
with a universal spirituality not limited to things as we
have always known them. To worship 'in spirit' is to
worship 'in truth'. A failure to widen our spiritual
horizons to see what God himself is doing in others and
is seeking to do in us may make us feel secure, but it is
not spiritual. The claim that 'this is the church' is not
always the expression of a spiritual worshipper but
often comes instead from a limited perception of what
God is doing throughout the world, merely revealing
feelings of insecurity about things we do not fully
understand or wish to learn about. Usually the outcome
is the same: we close off from new possibilities and
become an exclusive spiritual society, erecting barriers
that outsiders must pass before they can worship with
us.

With the proper safeguards it is possible to open the
windows without letting in the flies! A church with an
opened mind and heart will take care not to use
the language of privacy in public worship. In a post-
Christian society there are many visitors who may not
understand talk about 'the blood-washed saints' or 'the
old ship of Zion'. 'Justification', 'sanctification' and
'regeneration' are indispensable to Christian vocabulary
but may have little meaning to the average newcomer.
By opening the windows of our worship we deliberately
consider alternatives to 'church-talk' and to versions of
the Bible besides the AV. We have a willingness both to
hear what the Spirit *has said* to the churches but also
what he *is now saying* to the church today.

Such an openness should foster neither a careless

disregard for biblical truth, nor the abandonment of the hallmarks of true Pentecostalism. It is possible to have liberty without licence. Biblical holiness and the Spirit of Pentecost come to give life, not to suffocate. Pentecost seeks to enhance and not to entrench the believer. As the saying goes, 'Organisations which get stuck in a groove will never make records.' The latent power of many black churches has never truly been realised, for there is still a great task to be accomplished in releasing individuals and churches into a degree of spiritual maturity seldom seen. The great strides of black Pentecostalism in the UK over the last thirty years should not be regarded as its own reward; rather it should serve as a sobering indication of the potential in the black church community, as yet awaiting greater expression.

The place of awe

The Holiness tradition of the black church emphasises the glory and grandeur of God. It comes close to the ideal of 'the Holy Other' and tends towards an image of a God who is both present and removed. Pentecostalism celebrates a God who is 'closer than a brother', yet somehow mysterious in his holy otherness. The sense of awe so often missing among evangelicals or charismatics is, therefore, preserved in the tradition. It is sustained through the prayer language, the strong moral code and strident anti-sin slogans from the pulpit.

One of the main conveyors of the idea of the divine presence is the altar call. In the black church the altar is not the place of sacrament but rather the place of consecration. It is unusual not to have an altar call either for Christian commitment or for personal ministry. The altar may be as crude as a cushion on the floor, the seat of a chair or a pew; but it is always in the proximity of the pulpit and relates to the preached word. Phoebe Palmer, the American evangelist, was the first Pentecostal to install the altar call as an integral concept and practice of Pentecostalism; and, on the whole, black churches have remained true to that distinctive. As a church member insisted, 'You cannot have a church without an altar!' This Old Testament echo speaks of radical commitment in terms of time, talent and selfhood. A popular hymn expresses it well:

Is your all on the altar of sacrifice laid?
Your heart, does the Spirit control?
You can only be blessed
And have peace and sweet rest
As you yield him your body and soul.

The altar is also the place of deliverance. It is here that believers are called to receive healing or a ministry of consolation with the laying on of hands. This type of ministry, common to all Pentecostals, is the liturgical celebration of a God who *is* and who is actively involved with the triumphs and traumas of the people.

Bishop Patrick Kalilombe has identified two broad categories of worship: one that centres on the Bible and preaching ('the pulpit'); the other on the sacraments and rituals ('the altar').[13] In broad terms this is a useful means of identification, but Pentecostalism has a tendency to blend both the sacramentalism of the altar concept and the Nonconformism of the pulpit emphasis by its mastery of the spiritual language. Both preaching and Communion are vital in Pentecostalism, but pulpit and altar are basically utilitarian. The pulpit concept equates to the supremacy of the word, but the lectern is merely the place on which the preacher puts his Bible.

The altar concept represents radical response and commitment to discipleship, but the altar itself may only be a crude cushion on the floor. Both concepts are held together in a symbolic reality through the believer's faith. Pentecostalism provides a unique theological code in this synthesis of sacramental and Nonconformist tradition which brings altar and pulpit together by the language of faith.

Black Pentecostal worship has a degree of liberty which has been the focus of attention for many years. Though it is not a liturgical performance, it does issue from the liberating experience of the Spirit that is the hallmark of Pentecostalism. However, this freedom has been enhanced by the fact that the Afro-Caribbean culture has largely bypassed the Euro-centric inhibitions of rationalism which came out of the eighteenth-century Enlightenment and cast doubts on the validity of emotional involvement in worship. This is not of course to say that black Christians are non-rational, but the survival of black people over the last three hundred years has necessarily been the survival of the human spirit. Consequently the *soul* of the people rather than *reasoning* of the people has been the dominant feature.

This 'survival theology' had lodged itself deep within the heart of black church worship, particularly in the United States and the Caribbean. It has been the driving force behind the heavy emphasis on future salvation so present in much of the worship. Celebration and anticipation have therefore contributed healing properties to black worship.

Songs, sermons and prayers about heaven certainly provided a legitimate diversion from the toils of grinding poverty, exploitation or educational disadvantage, but they did not act as an *escape* from reality. Rather, heaven made reality bearable. In the face of racism, marginalisation, poverty and ignorance, there was no analysis of suffering—simply an experience of pain, for which there was no rational explanation. Heaven offered the only grounds for optimism in a world where black people worked a lot and owned very little. This hope offered a greater reality, bestowed a sense of worth and made them 'not ashamed'. We are not ashamed of who we are because we have a hope.

Pentecostalism holds on to the awe of God because of its theology of *transcendent immanence*. This means that there is a two-edged belief: that God is above all things, yet also present in that sovereignty. This theology is reinforced by the strong commitment to the belief in the imminent return of Jesus Christ at the Rapture. Many Pentecostals still begin their letters with 'greetings in the name of Jesus, our soon-coming King'.

Such an unshaken expectation motivates the black Pentecostal to stay on the right side of grace—prepared for the Rapture. In its earliest stages the fathers of modern Pentecostalism unfurled the theology of the Rapture—that Jesus' return would be an instantaneous and decisive gathering of the true church out of the world (1 Thess 4:13 – 5:4). The Rapture is therefore an important component of the pre-millennial doctrine of Pentecostalism (see Rev 20). This, briefly stated, is that Jesus will return to take the true church to himself before returning to reign on the earth for a thousand years. At the end of that time, all the powers of evil will be subjected to him in the cataclysmic battle of Armageddon, when righteousness will finally triumph over evil.

The pre-millennium Second Coming of Christ is not only important in terms of its demand for constant

ethical and moral vigilance. It also confronts the worshipper with the omnipotence of a God who is able to
determine the scale and conclusion of human history.
The God to whom all knees must bow in a final act of
total submission (Rev 20:11–15) is a God worth
worshipping *now*! Black Pentecostal worship is greatly
enhanced by this immanence, which is not only for
the Last Days but also for today! Indeed, black
Pentecostalism worships in the conviction that today
belongs to the Last Days. As a result, the worship may
be perceived as eschatological worship for it rejoices in
a 'soon-coming King' who is not a millennium away but
'just behind the door'. Effectively, worship today is
therefore a part of the account of the Last Days; it is
worshipping in the light of the Kingdom rather than the
shadow of the past. This is why the worship and
interaction of black church experience can be so powerful. Song leaders know this not by theological insight
but by theological intuition and so challenge the worshippers to come together in the Spirit. 'If we can't
worship together down here,' they will ask, 'how are
you going to worship with us in heaven?'

As Carlton Pearson, the Black American preacher,
exclaimed, 'I'm glad I've got a God I can feel!' That God
who is present must also be present to work. Black
Pentecostalism believes in a God who is felt and who
acts tangibly on our behalf. To that extent it is therefore
an empirical belief-system—it actually expects 'signs to
follow' and believes in 'spiritual results'. Certainly, in
its earlier stages black churches would be devastated if
no one returned from a national meeting without some
identifiable indications of God's action on the church's
behalf. Worship is, therefore, the celebration of a God
who *is* but also of a God who *does*, and good preaching

is judged by the visible response to the good news, resulting in a worship commitment at the altar.

Such is the power of Pentecost; not only has it given hope for the future; in the process it has also given preservation in the present. That staying power cannot properly be understood merely in sociological terms, for it is essentially the work of the Spirit in the spirit of the people expressed in the excitement of the worship. It is not false hope but 'lively hope' celebrated in song:

The victory that I have
The world can't give it to me.
The victory that I have
The world can't give it to me.
The victory that I have
The world can't give it to me.
The world don't have it,
The world can't give it,
The world can't take it away.

Today a part of the transition of black church worship is the gradual disappearance of this eschatological emphasis. The new generation of British black Christians have emerged with the tools of social analysis and a sense of belonging to their environment. For them, heaven is still real, though not urgent. Relatively few of the gospel songs reflect the 'Beaulah land' of their spiritual parents. The search is for a liturgy which is *relevant* and *relational*: a worship setting with words and music which celebrates the lordship of Christ within contemporary situations. The silent but significant transition goes unnoticed: it has less preoccupation with tomorrow.

Although this is not the whole story, black Pentecostalism is indeed inseparable from an understanding of black worship generally. It has its own distinct characteristics, history and challenges. It has emerged from the Holiness code of nineteenth-century North America and has been impregnated by intuitive Africanisms in the USA and Caribbean. Even in the midst of significant changes it still maintains an infectious and vibrant reality. As John Root explains it, 'When you have visited a black Pentecostal church, you know you have been to church.'[14]

Notes

1. Lennox Powell was speaking at the Association of Full Gospel Churches, Kingston, Jamaica, in November 1990.
2. Revd Dr Iain MacRobert 'Black to the Future' ACEA Youth Network Conference, Birmingham 20th April 1991.
3. Chuck Wagon Gang was a popular American group which influenced black church choirs during the 1950s to 1970s.
4. This story raises an interesting debate for which we do not have scope in this chapter, but it is Vinson Synon who credits Mary Campbell with this distinction in *In the Latter Days* (Servant Publications: Michigan, 1984), p 33. On the other hand, Andrew Walker's more recent work gives the point to Mrs Catherine Price from Brixton, who was alleged to be the first tongue-speaking person in British Pentecostalism, in 1907. *Restoring the Kingdom* (Hodder & Stoughton: London, 1989), p 248.
5. Donald Gee, *Wind and Flame* (Assemblies of God Publishing House: London, 1967), p 86.
6. Charles Conn, *Like a Mighty Army* (Pathway Press, 1977), p 8.

7. Ira Brooks, *Another Gentleman to the Ministry* (Compeer Press: Birmingham).

8. Io Smith, *An Ebony Cross* (Marshalls, 1989).

9. 63rd General Assembly of Church of God, San Antonio, Texas (7–12 August 1990).

10. Colin Whittaker, *Seven Pentecostal Pioneers* (Marshall Pickering, 1986), p 164.

11. An examination of some Old Testament texts (Gen 18: 4–5; 19:2–3; 24:32–33; 43:24–25; Judg 19:21) all show footwashing linked to domestic hospitality and taking place before a meal. The assertion that John 13 was only related to Eastern hospitality and hygiene must be used with some caution if viewed in the light of these texts.

12. Andrew Walker, *Restoring the Kingdom* (Hodder & Stoughton: London, 1989), p 50.

13. Bishop Patrick Kalilombe, 'The Altar and the Pulpit' a lecture delivered at the Centre for Black and White Partnership, Birmingham, 4th May 1991.

14. John Root 'Encountering West Indian Pentecostalism' (Grove Booklet No 66, 1979), p 20.

5

The Interaction Between Culture and Worship

Len Anglin

Having looked at worship with the Afro-Caribbean setting, it would be useful to reflect briefly on what we mean by the idea of 'culture'.

Reflections on culture

Richard Niebuhr in his work *Christ and Culture* states that the task of defining 'culture' can only be undertaken in a tenuous fashion, especially when this definition is attempted in a Christian context:

> A theologian's definition of the term must, in the nature of the case, be a layman's definition, since he cannot presume to enter into the issues raised by professional anthropologists. Yet it must also, at least initially, be a definition of the phenomenon without theological interpretation, for it is just this theological interpretation which is the point of issue among Christians.[1]

According to Niebuhr, culture is the artificial secondary environment that man superimposes on the natural. It comprises language, habits, ideas, beliefs, customs, social organisation, inherited artifacts, technical processes and values. For him, culture is quite distinct from the natural order of created things. Effectively it is a synthetic environment created by people over a long period of time.[2]

John Stott regards culture as an amalgam of beliefs, values, customs, and institutions developed by each society and transmitted to the next generation: it is the complement of nature. What is natural is God-given and inherited; what is cultural is 'man-made' and learned.[3]

Other views on culture include the concept of an integrated system of learned patterns of behaviour, ideas, and products characteristic of a society;[4] all non-material traits passed on from one generation to another;[5] the system of beliefs, values, customs, and institutions which bind a society together and give it a sense of identity;[6] the system of shared meanings developed in a particular social and economic context.[7]

At the Afro-Caribbean Evangelical Alliance Theological Study Group it was agreed that culture, by its various definitions seems to be 'one's way of living; that which has formed one's being. This includes factors such as language, experience, food, music, and history.'[8]

There is a variety of cultures in the world. If we understand that God has made every nation to inherit the earth in different places, then the fact of a variety of cultures has to be accepted and appreciated.

The wonder of worship

It is safe to say that human beings were created with the basic desire and need to worship, which can of course be understood in different ways. Though this point has been made in previous chapters, it will be amplified for emphasis in this chapter. Our main focus here will be the specific aspect of corporate worship in the local church setting.

In worship there is a close relationship between being and doing. Ronald Ward states:

Worship may be briefly described as an adoring mental attitude toward God and an outward expression in corporate speech and act. It recognises God's holiness, goodness and love and reverently tells God so. Apart from the fact that worship is divinely commended ('Thou shalt worship the Lord thy God' [Matt 4:10]), it has an inherent reasonableness. If God is utter perfection, then he ought to be praised.[9]

In fact a closer examination of Revelation 4:10–11 reveals how true worship can be brought to the most Worthy One. The twenty-four elders around the throne of God prostrate themselves before the royal ruler on the throne. They worship the eternal One and give up their own glory (crowns) to him. They declare his worthship ('Thou art worthy') as the Creator of all things. This is the central thought in worship.[10]

The essence of true worship, then, is the celebration of God. It is not a casual or careless venture but is carried out with as much thought as that which goes into the planning and celebrating of a birthday or anniversary. It does not consist of gifts given grudgingly or out of compulsion but with delight (2 Cor 9:7). It does not encompass haphazard music poorly done or merely performed but music offered with joy and spirit, as Psalm 100 urges. It is an active response to God whereby we are not passive spectators but active participants. Worship is not something we watch or that is done for us but something we do.[11]

Corporate worship in the Bible

The Old Testament shows clearly the centrality of the worship of Jahweh, the God of Israel, in national life; but it hardly provides us with any full description of one such act of worship, whether an isolated sacrifice or a major festival in Jerusalem.

> Some special orders of service are described, e.g., Solomon's dedication of the temple (II Chron 5–7), and certain stipulations about the way in which sacrifices should be offered are given (Lev 6–7), but we do not see the whole picture with spoken liturgy, ceremonial action, and detailed rubrics all included.[12]

The New Testament also says little about the form and content of worship in the local church, though passages such as Acts 2, Acts 20, 1 Corinthians 12–14, and 1 Thessalonians 5:16 do provide us with an idea of the order of service followed in the early church.

Preaching

Preaching is declaring God's word as recorded in the Bible. This aspect of worship received priority attention according to the Old and New Testament accounts of contemporary worship. Preaching in the sense of interpreting the Bible was unknown in Judaism until after the Babylonian exile. The Hebrew prophets were preachers, but they were primarily exhorters, interpreters of the will of God, not preachers of the Scriptures, since the Bible as we know it was not yet available as the authoritative word of God. In the early church the Old Testament Scriptures were held in high regard and were thus publicly read (1 Tim 4:13), along with Paul's epistles (1 Thess 5:27). The word was also preached to win converts and to build up believers (Acts 2:41; 4:4).

Prayer

Adoration and supplication in prayer were elements which dominated Old Testament worship. The progressive revelation by God, culminating with the Incarnation of Jesus Christ, meant that prayer in worship carried different forms. The role of the priest in the Old Testament was important in the experience of worshippers, for he was the mediator between God and the people. As he was their direct point of reference, without him they could not worship God. By contrast, the New Testament provision through Jesus Christ has made prayer more direct and personal to the worshippers. Christ is now the High Priest, the Mediator between God and human beings.

Music

Expression in music was another feature of Old Testament worship, as the Psalms clearly prove. The use of a variety of instruments in worship was commonplace and expected, for the Bible makes reference to several instruments of praise in the giving of thanks to God.

When Moses led Israel out of Egypt, for example, he paused to praise God in song (Exod 15:1–18). Miriam the prophetess led all the women in music and dance (Exod 15:20). Other examples include Deborah's song of victory (Judg 5) and David dancing before the Lord (2 Sam 6:14). Nehemiah's account states that they worshipped 'at the dedication of the wall of Jerusalem . . . with gladness . . . with thanksgivings, and with singing, with cymbals, psalteries, and with harps' (Neh 12:27). The story continues in chapter 12 with some of the priests' sons going before the people with trumpets (v 35) with the musical instruments of David and with Ezra the scribe (v 36). The priests blew the trumpets (v 41) and the singers sang loudly (v 42) and all the people offered great sacrifices and rejoiced (v 43).

The Psalms are replete with instances of and exhortations to praise God—with singing, with the instruments, and with clapping. In biblical times the children of Israel sang the Psalms to the accompaniment of harps and other stringed instruments. 'Be thou exalted, Lord, in thine own strength: so will we sing and praise thy power' (Ps 21:13). Psalm 81 exhorts: 'Sing aloud unto God our strength: make a joyful noise unto the God of Jacob. Take a psalm, and bring hither the timbrel, the pleasant harp with the psaltery. Blow up the trumpet in the new moon, in the time appointed, on our solemn feast day (vv 1–3).

Psalm 87 refers to the singers as well as the players on instruments who will be there in the new world when the Lord shall 'count' his people. Psalm 126 relates the rescue from captivity accompanied by laughter and singing. Psalm 135:3 encourages the singing of praises unto God. Psalm 144:9 says: 'I will sing a new song unto thee, O God: upon a psaltery and an instrument of ten strings will I sing praises unto thee.'

In the New Testament the disciples sang in the Upper Room (Mk 14:26). Paul instructed believers to sing psalms, hymns and spiritual songs (Eph 5:18–20). He and Silas sang praises in prison at midnight (Acts 16:25). That the redeemed will sing in heaven is foretold in Revelation 15:3.

Giving

Both the Old and New Testaments stress the need for giving to God to be an active part of worship. In the Old Testament, tithing, which is the giving of the tenth of one's material goods, was an important aspect of Jewish life and worship. The various offerings that were required were above and beyond the tithe.

The New Testament says more about giving than about any other single aspect of church life. The reference to a weekly allocation in 1 Corinthians 16:2, the liturgical significance given to a financial gift to Paul (Phil 4:10–18), and mention of an offering in patristic writings have led to the view that an offering was a basic element in Christian worship. Liberality was taught as part of serving God (2 Cor 8:14; 1 Tim 5:17–18).[13]

Spiritual gifts and the Lord's Supper

The manifestation of various gifts of the Spirit was a real part of worship, too. In the New Testament Paul's first epistle to the Corinthians is the clearest indication that it was normal for the spiritual gifts to be manifest in worship. The historical record of the Book of Acts convinces us that the celebration of the Lord's Supper was also a regular part of the weekly corporate experience.

Mono-cultural worship

There has been considerable debate in recent years about whether a local church could or ever should be culturally homogeneous. Is it possible to assert simultaneously the unity of the human race through Jesus Christ and the diversity of ethnic cultures? In other words, since God has brought us into his new society, he is therefore calling us into a new internationalism. But does this obliterate our nationality? (The issue is not just a black culture versus a white culture. 'Multi-cultural' transcends a black-white distinction, embracing the entire range of cultural diversities.)

On the one hand, Bible texts such as Galatians 3:28— 'There is neither Jew nor Greek . . . for ye are all one in Christ'—seem to state that cultural distinctions are provided for in the body of Christ. Accordingly, an intermix of cultures in a local church, and in particular in local church worship, is both desirable and healthy. National, racial, social, and gender distinctions remain, but individuals are brought as they are into the body of Christ, and these distinctions no longer divide us.

Since the New Jerusalem will be enriched by the colourful 'mosaic of human cultures', there is indeed room for the present intermix of cultures (Rev 21:24–26). John Benington points out that no man's land is God's land, and that there are fresh things to learn from him in every culture.[14] God is no stranger to cultures different from our own; therefore all should be brought together so that individuals can be enriched. Acts 6:1–7 provides an example of a multi-cultural local church where a variety of cultures *was* catered for.

On the other hand, it may be argued that this intermix of cultures in a local church is deeply problematic. Each race has the right to preserve its culture as manifested in—and as it affects—worship. In many cases these cultural features are opposed to and vastly different from each other; it therefore makes it impossible and impractical for them to merge in a common worship experience. Language is one obvious barrier, since people worship most comfortably and effectively in their first language. In order to give the most to and get the most from worship, therefore, the individual needs to worship using that first language. But within the same language there are difficulties in aiming for a mono-cultural church. Turns of phrase, diction and slang all differ within a culture, even among those who speak the same language, and can hinder meaningful worship. If we have to spend too much time trying to hear and understand what is said, worship may become less than meaningful.

While mutual trust and confidence are essential ingredients in worship, a variety of cultures in the same worship may undermine them, since people tend to be more at ease with others of their own culture, and peculiarities and preferences in individuals are best appreciated by those of the same culture. Tension in worship and church life is reduced, then, with a monocultural church. Galatians 3:28 is probably best understood as applying to the church as an organic body rather than to the local church. Prejudice and hatred based on cultural differences are eradicated because of the blood of Jesus; this is the oneness referred to in the text.

Young black British Christians

With the establishment of the black churches in Britain, parents were able to find the type of worship they enjoyed, and which provided them with spiritual strength and stability. God was made real through worship.

Literally they were able to sing 'the Lord's song in a strange land'. They found what they had left 'back home', and gained spiritual strength in worshipping by 'association', motivated by memories of worship experiences 'back home'. Quite naturally, the worship experience took the form of the culture from which they came.

Young black British Christians today, however, face a serious dilemma: they find it difficult to appreciate the worship patterns and practices of the culture of their parents, yet are equally unable to identify with the worship patterns and practices of the UK culture in which they were born or brought up. This clash has led in my experience to a complete rejection of Christianity in many instances.

Young blacks in the UK find it very difficult to appreciate the same aspects of worship which clearly provide solace, comfort, direction and satisfaction for their parents. In many cases they have been forced to attend worship and were taken to church for every activity. Of course these parents meant well. Most came from a culture where the church was central and where church involvement was at once a religious and a social phenomenon, a view inevitably transferred to Britain. Such parents saw it necessary and important to attend church as regularly as they could. Often, too, financial restrictions forced them to take their children with them to every church function, especially since they were unable to pay baby sitters. The overriding factor, however, was that the parents considered church attendance and involvement compulsory for their children. Meanwhile since they had not been exposed to the particular experiences of their parents, young people have not been as motivated by or attracted to their parents' type of worship pattern, in many instances finding it irrelevant and tedious.

In such circumstances young blacks have found it difficult to appreciate certain standards set by their parents. Some of these standards, as I will state later in the chapter, were framed more by cultural factors than by biblical teachings. Comments such as 'I have had too much church during my childhood,' indicate just how alienated these youths and young adults feel about the obviously honest and well-intentioned efforts of their parents. The dilemma is that these individuals have been caught between cultures. Despite the fact that there are some young black British who have been able to identify with white Pentecostal churches, these are in the minority.

Challenges in multi-cultural local worship

Since there is such a close relationship between 'being' and 'doing' in worship, it is quite clear that we cannot divorce our culture from our worship. It does not require much stretching of the imagination, however, to picture what could happen if no controls were placed on the extent to which all cultures were accommodated in worship. To avoid confusion, certain points need to be understood and applied.

Culture is a means to an end, not an end in itself, and as such it needs to be seen in proper perspective in worship. Cultural factors must therefore not be confused with biblical standards; in fact, culture must be subject to biblical authority. This is critical.

In the New Testament we find many examples of violations in worship. With the birth of the Christian church and new-found liberty in Christ came the tension between 'preserving' and 'violating'. Early Jewish Christians faced this tension perhaps more than any other group. In Acts 15 we find a glaring show-down. On one hand, those who were influenced and governed all their lives by the practice of Jewish circum-cision could not visualise true worship of God without it. On the other hand, Jesus made it clear that what was necessary now was the circumcision of the heart. This resulted in a major conflict in the Jerusalem Church.

Later, the newly converted Christians in Corinth, whose value systems and practice included the eating of meat offered to idols, faced a similar dilemma. The pagan culture to which they had been exposed gave credence to various pagan festivals. Having now found a new faith which denounced these previously accepted normal practices, the Corinthian Christians needed some guidelines. Paul's answer indicates a number of things, especially that practices which encourage idolatry cannot be followed by Christians:

> What say I then? that the idol is any thing, or that which is offered in sacrifice to idols is any thing?
>
> But I say, that the things which the Gentiles sacrifice, they sacrifice to devils, and not to God: and I would not that ye should have fellowship with devils.
>
> Ye cannot drink the cup of the Lord, and the cup of devils; ye cannot be partakers of the Lord's table, and of the table of devils (1 Cor 10:19–21).

The urgency of the issues means that Christians must confront cultural practices which may exclude others and inhibit the growth of the local church. The truly born-again Christian—Paul argues in verses 23–33—would know how to sacrifice previously dearly held rights and privileges for the spiritual welfare of others.

In our own time, the situation has been equally complex and sensitive. A study of missions and missionary activities will reveal a number of atrocities. Whether knowingly or ignorantly, certain cultural values were transmitted to receiving cultures as if they were part of the faith. But many standards accepted as biblical were in fact cultural. Perhaps the most glaring example of this is in the matter of dress. Where certain attire was necessary because of the climatic and social conditions in some countries, it was taken and even taught as a biblical norm in countries where such attire was utterly inappropriate. The colonial system and practice certainly did not help in this regard.

Fortunately, since the start of the twentieth century, with so many countries achieving their independence, some values and value systems came under strict review. The Christian church in these lands, not to be outdone by society in general, also re-examined a number of its practices in and requirements for worship. Correct and consistent biblical interpretation revealed many mal-practices. Many countries have therefore undertaken a major review of the mode of dress and attire for worship. It has become increasingly clear that in this regard many churches were teaching as commandments the doctrines of men.

All this is not to overlook the enlightenment that many cultures have received from the activities and ministry of missionaries. Many previously accepted cultural practices, when examined under the light of biblical truth taught by sincere missionaries, were clearly condemned. Human sacrifice as a part of worship is one such practice, which was accepted by many cultures as normal and necessary—clearly a viola-tion of the biblical commandment 'Thou shalt not commit murder.' The central point, in any case, is that cultural factors, no matter how 'sacred' they may be, must not be confused with Bible standards.

The influence of culture on the biblical pattern and standard for worship needs to be analysed. Since human beings are shaped by varying cultural factors, and since worship involves our whole identity it follows that worship modes will vary according to their cultural context.

The length of worship needs to be addressed, espe-cially as the response to time varies from culture to culture. In some cultures the emphasis is on the nature of the occasion. This means that little notice is paid to the clock. In other cultures, punctuality, brevity, and precision become key factors in worship. The situation is all the more delicate because the Bible does not give clear directions in this regard. The freedom in the Spirit which the Bible speaks about is used as justification for worship without time restriction, while others understand that the Bible expects everything to be done 'decently and in order'—so time becomes important.

The declaration of the Holy Scriptures has already been regarded as an undisputed aspect of biblical worship. The content of the Holy Scriptures is objectively sound and therefore inflexible; even misinterpretations of Scripture do not change the objective validity of the word. Homiletics (simply, the art of preaching), relates directly to the declaration of the Holy Scriptures. The style of the preacher is important to the extent that it helps to prepare and subsequently to open the minds of the hearers to the ideas developed in the sermon.

Clearly, then, both preacher and hearers influenced by cultural factors need to exercise sensitivity to each other. Though the Scriptures command sincerity of life and soundness of doctrine for effective preaching, they do not dictate the manner and style. 'Anointed preaching' is what is required.

What is anointed preaching? Individual cultures would no doubt be tempted to insist that their own particular style of preaching is anointed—an assertion which would be correct, providing that the basic prerequisites for anointed preaching were met; for sincerity of life and soundness of doctrine transcend culture. Clearly, anointed preaching is not determined *by* culture but perceived *through* culture and merely enhanced by cultural factors.

Adoration and supplication in prayer are vital aspects of corporate worship. Cultural factors would therefore greatly influence such a personal act and experience of prayer, and this is where the internal and external features of prayer meet. We can best understand these aspects as we follow the line of Jesus' teaching on prayer in the gospels; he warned against show and hypocrisy in prayer (Lk 18:9–14). Communication with God is the essential of prayer. As long as this is achieved, it hardly matters how this is done culturally.

Musical expression is arguably the most controversial aspect of public worship, partly because it *is* so affected by culture. Barton Babbage gives effective guidelines here:

> The purpose of worship is expressed in the succinct words of the Psalmist: 'Give unto the Lord the glory due unto his name; worship the Lord in the beauty of holiness' (29:2 cf. 96:9). Thus the primary purpose of worship is not moral uplift, nor ecstatic feeling, nor aesthetic pleasure; on the contrary, worship means giving to God that of which he is worthy (the root word means 'worthship'), that which is his due. This provides us with the criterion by which to judge the propriety of traditional and accepted aids to worship. The question which we must ask is this: Do they give glory to God? Do they enable us to worship the Lord in the beauty of holiness?[15]

So the appropriate place of music in the activity of public worship cannot be ignored. Individuals of various cultural backgrounds will be affected by different types of music. As a motivator in worship, then, musical variety has to be appreciated. The expressions that accompany the music will vary as much as the music itself, according to culture. In the words of Babbage, if music is to aid worship, it must be 'modest, not flamboyant; it must be genuinely congregational and serve the cause of truth and edification'.[16]

Showing appreciation of God's goodness in congregational giving, exercise of various gifts of the Spirit and celebration of the Lord's Supper have been as much affected by cultural factors as preaching, prayer and music. However, since arguments on these aspects of worship have been more theological than cultural, we'll set them aside here.

Questions to the black church and a possible way forward

Whatever our definition of the black church, certain direct questions need to be answered by those of us whose culture differs from that of British whites. Have black churches, by the style of worship, undermined the culture into which they have settled? Is the black church guilty of 'reversed stereotypical condemnation'? Has the black church overreacted? By its insistence on maintaining certain styles of worship, has the black church excluded white worshippers from its congregations? Has the black church limited the universality of the gospel by undermining or ignoring other cultures?

Is the black church guilty of equating emotionalism with Spirit-filled worship? Does the black church admit that orthodox, quiet and staid worship is also acceptable to God? Does the black church recognise that certain aspects of worship—hand-clapping, dancing, the use of musical instruments, vocal expressions of rejoicing—are not cultural? And what is the black church doing for and about children born or brought up in a culture different from that of their parents; children who are caught between cultures?

We obviously cannot ignore the black church's experience of racial prejudice in earlier years—an especially painful experience for its members. The initial rejection that black worshippers faced in those days has surely left its scars. Perhaps it can be argued that initially there was no attempt to exclude white worshippers from black churches. The intention was simply to provide for the worshipping black church community. But with the rise in Pentecostalism, and in particular the charismatic groups, it has become increasingly clear that styles of worship previously labelled 'black' are in fact biblical and non-cultural or 'a-cultural'. It is also true that the intensity with which these styles of worship is executed is indeed subject to cultural factors, since the more expressive and open nature of the black culture certainly influences worship. But the black church, in seeking suitable worshipping environs, never deliberately excluded the white worshippers on racial grounds.

One recognises that perceptions are crucial, as we seek to answer the various questions posed. Perhaps the black church cannot claim total innocence. Perhaps various churches and individuals have overreacted to the racism and prejudice that they have encountered.

With the rapid changes in the society, the black church is becoming more aware of its role, now seeking to answer questions that were previously neither urgent nor relevant. The black church's participation in churches' fraternals, in joint services and programmes indicates the stage at which we are now. The black church makes no claim of exclusivism. In fact, some of the features of the so-called 'black worship' have been accepted and are being sought after by white worshippers and by the established British churches. The Holy Spirit's work in bridging gaps and in illuminating and enlightening is of great significance in the way.

In spite of the human element which has often thwarted the work of the Spirit, God has gone on bringing together true worshippers from varying cultures and races. However, there is still a long way to go. The black church will have to remain open to the healing power of the Holy Spirit. It will continually have to put history and experience in proper perspective, for history and experience should be tools for progress rather than excuses for separation. Conversely, white worshippers need to rise above the still-existing pressures from the society. In their quest for God they need to see the God of *all* cultures. While the black church actively plays its role in bridging the gaps between cultures, it cannot afford to do so at the expense of its own culture.

The call for tolerance and love would therefore be appropriate, and honesty and relevance are equally essential. The young black British Christian raises a special challenge for today's older black Christian.

The brutal fact is that the generations of black people who came to Britain had the advantage of exposure to their own peculiar culture and environs. These experiences stayed with them and served as a buffer in the crisis of adjustment to a new culture. By contrast, the children born or brought up in Britain have been exposed to a variety of cultures. As we have already identified, this has posed problems for young people as they seek to worship the Lord. The question then to the black church becomes crucially important: what are we doing for them?

May I suggest some courses of action we need to take

if the black church is to be of relevance to young people in crisis? First of all, the black church will need to be more precise in distinguishing cultural from biblical factors in worship. We owe it to our children to give them a rationale for our faith, one that is at once true to timeless Bible truths *and* relevant to the present realities. The gospel therefore has to be presented as far as possible without the distortions and trappings of culture, with encouragement to young people to apply it to culture so that those young people will then be free to develop and express their own culture. This may well be a hybrid of the two cultures, but it will clearly be their own, and it will certainly influence their approach to worship. Whatever type of worship results, parents of these young people and the black church as a whole will have to respect it and accept it as given unto God.

Secondly, the black church must allow for young people to fill leadership roles within the church—responsibilities and authority. As in all cases, the Bible has to be the yardstick for measuring their effectiveness, as well as a willingness on the part of older members to avoid the eight dying words of a church: 'We have never done it that way before.'

The challenge to the black church is both complicated and great, external and internal. True worship of God will result when as a church we are honest and open to God, to others, and to ourselves.

Notes

1. Niebuhr, Richard, *Christ and Culture* (Harper & Row: New York, 1975), p 30.
2. *Ibid*, p 32.
3. Stott, John, 'Involvement', *Social and Sexual Relation-*

ships in the Modern World, Vol. II (Fleming H. Revell: New Jersey, 1984), p 91.

4. Hiebert, as cited by Eddie Gibbs, *I Believe in Church Growth* (Hodder & Stoughton: London, 1981).

5. Nida, Eugene, *Customs, Culture and Christianity* (Tyndale, 1954).

6. Willowbank, as cited by Eddie Gibbs, *op cit*.

7. Saifullah, Khan V, 'The Role of the Culture of Dominance in Structuring the Experience of Ethnic Minorities', *Race in Britain: Continuity and Change* (Hutchinson Educational, 1979).

8. Afro-Caribbean Evangelical Alliance Theological Study Group: December 1989.

9. Ward, Ronald A, 'The New Testament Basis', *Baker's Dictionary of Practical Theology*, Ed. Ralph G. Turnbull (Baker Book House: Grand Rapids, 1967), p 364.

10. *Growing Toward Spiritual Maturity* (Evangelical Theological Training Association: Wheaton, 1988), p 47.

11. *Ibid*, p 48.

12. Taylor, J.B., 'The Old Testament Background', *Baker's Dictionary of Practical Theology*, Ed. Ralph G. Turnbull (Baker Book House: Grand Rapids, 1967), p 373.

13. Evangelical Theological Training Association, *op cit*, p 51.

14. Benington, John, *Culture, Class and Christian Beliefs* (Scripture Union, 1974).

15. Babbage, Barton, 'Aids to Worship', *Baker's Dictionary of Practical Theology* (Baker Book House, 1967), p 401.

16. *Ibid*.

Bibliography

Benington, John. *Culture, Class and Christian Beliefs.* Scripture Union, 1974.

Brooks, Ira V. *Another Gentleman to the Ministry.* Compeer Press Ltd: Birmingham.

Calley, Malcolm J.C. *God's People: West Indian Pentecostal Sects in England.* Oxford University Press: London, 1965.

Charman, Paul. *Reflections, Black and White Christians in the City.* Zebra Project: London, 1979.

Church of God in Black Perspective, The. Proceedings of the Caucus of Black Churchmen in the Church of God: Cleveland, Ohio, April 1970.

Cone, James. *God of the Oppressed.* SPCK: London, 1977.

Douglas, J.D. *The New Bible Dictionary.* InterVarsity Press: London.

Faith in the City. A report of the Archbishop of Canterbury's Commission on Urban Priority Areas: London, 1986.

Foner, Eric. *America's Black Past.* Harper & Row: New York, 1970.

Gates, Brian. *Afro-Caribbean Religions.* London, 1980.

Gerloff, Roswith. *Partnership between Black and White.* Methodist Home Mission: London, 1977.

Gibbs, E. *I Believe in Church Growth.* Hodder & Stoughton: London, 1954.

Growing Toward Spiritual Maturity. Evangelical Teacher Training Association: Wheaton, Illinois, 1988.

Haines, Lee. *An Outline History of the Wesleyan Church.* Wesley Press, 1976.

Hamilton, Charles. *The Black Preacher in America*. William Morrow & Co Inc: New York, 1972.

Holden, Tony. *People, Churches and Multi-Racial Projects*. The Methodist Church Division of Social Responsibility, 1984.

Hollenweger, Walter J. *The Pentecostals*. London, 1972.

Howard, Venessa. *A Report on Afro-Caribbean Christianity in Britain*. Community Religious Project: Leeds University, 1987.

Jackson, Anita. *Catching Both Sides of the Wind; conversations with five black pastors*. The British Council of Churches: Warrington, 1985.

Jones, Howard. *White Questions to a Black Christian*. Zondervan: Grand Rapids, 1975.

Leech, Kenneth. *Struggle in Babylon: racism in the cities and churches of Britain*. Sheldon Press: London, 1988.

Luscombe, Carmen. *The Black-Led Churches*.

Members One of Another: a study guide for a multi-racial church in a multi-racial society. Methodist Church Division of Social Responsibility, 1986.

Nida, Eugene A. *Message and Mission: The Communications of the Christian Faith*. William Carey Library: South Pasadena, 1960.

Niebuhr, H. Richard. *Christ and Culture*. Harper & Row: New York, 1975.

Rainbow Gospel. Report on Challenging Racism in Britain. The British Council of Churches Inter-Church House: Otley, West Yorkshire, 1988.

Shepherd, David. *Bias to the Poor*. London, 1985.

Smelser, Neil J. *Sociology: An Introduction*. New York, 1967.

Smith, Greg. 'Christian Ethnics'. British Church Growth Association: Harrow.

Spirituals and the Blues. Seaburn Press: New York, 1972.

Stott, John. 'Involvement'. *Being a Responsible Christian in a Non-Christian Society*. Vol. I. Fleming H. Revell: New Jersey, 1984.

Stott, John. 'Involvement'. *Social and Sexual Relationships in the Modern World*, Vol. II. Fleming H. Revell: New Jersey, 1984.

Synan, Vinson. *The Holiness-Pentecostal Movement in the United States*. Grand Rapids, 1971.

Turnbull, Ralph G. *Baker's Dictionary of Practical Theology*. Baker Book House: Grand Rapids, 1967.

Walter, Heather. *A Tree God Planted: Black People in British Methodism*. Ethnic Minorities in Methodism Working Group, 1985.

Walter, Williston. *A History of the Christian Church*. Edinburgh, 1976.

With you in the Spirit. Report of Cardinal Hume's Advisory Group on the Catholic Church's commitment to the Black Community. The Business Print Ltd.